pitman
2000
SHORTHAND

First Course
Second Edition

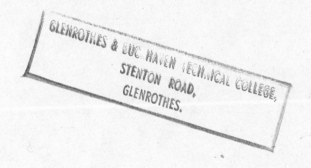

pitman 2000 SHORTHAND

First Course
Second Edition

Pitman

PITMAN BOOKS LIMITED
128 Long Acre, London, WC2E 9AN

Associated Companies
Pitman Publishing Pty Ltd, Melbourne
Pitman Publishing New Zealand Ltd, Wellington

© Pitman Books Limited 1982

First edition 1975
Second edition 1982
Reprinted 1982 (twice), 1983

Isaac Pitman

Text set in 10/12 pt Linotron 202 Bembo
Printed and bound in Great Britain at The Pitman Press, Bath

ISBN 0 273 01800 0

CONTENTS

PREFACE

Pitman 2000 Shorthand is a modified open-ended version of Pitman's Shorthand as it has been known and practised over the past fifty-nine years in its New Era form.

The modification was introduced to remove those sophisticated parts of the New Era form that are applicable only to small groups of words, and to dispense with those other devices which are not needed by today's office worker.

Pitman 2000 Shorthand has been deliberately devised with a light memory load to ensure easy mastery of the rules and accurate transcription with reduction in learning time.

This streamlined second edition of *Pitman 2000 Shorthand First Course* clearly defines and illustrates the rules of the system with graded exercise material following each rule.

The publishers are grateful for the many valuable suggestions from teachers and students worldwide following the publication of the first edition, and it is in response to a majority request that the longhand keys no longer appear in this text. A key is published separately for those who require it.

Before beginning work on Unit 1, careful reading of the Introduction which follows this preface is recommended, in order that the maximum benefit from your study of Pitman's Shorthand may be obtained.

INTRODUCTION

Pitman 2000 Shorthand represents spoken sounds by written signs. Writing by sound means writing words as they are pronounced and not according to longhand spelling. The following illustration shows how to think of words when writing shorthand:

palm	is	p-ah-m	caught	is	k-aw-t
pale	is	p-ay-l	bowl	is	b-oh-l
knee	is	n-ee	tomb	is	t-oo-m

Look at the words again, and their corresponding pronunciation, and note that:

(a) just as the spelling of words is made up of consonants and vowels; so too is their pronunciation;

(b) silent letters are not represented in the pronunciation, e.g., tom*b*, pa*l*m;

(c) generally speaking, there are fewer letters used to represent the pronunciation of words than the spelling, e.g., k-aw-t (caught).

In longhand the alphabet consists of consonants and vowels, combinations of which are used to form words. In Pitman's Shorthand signs are used to represent only those consonants and vowels which are actually sounded when pronouncing words. However, although the system is phonetic, it is not designed to represent or record minute shades of pronunciation. It does not seek to mark, for example, the thirty or more variations of sound which have been found to exist in the utterance of the twelve simple vowels. The pronunciation of the vowels varies greatly in different localities and in the various countries of the world in which the English language is spoken and in which Pitman's Shorthand is practised. The standard of pronunciation, as shown in printed shorthand, cannot, therefore, be the same as that in spoken English everywhere. However, for the sake of consistency it is essential to have a standard in which shorthand is printed so that it is not read in one form in one place and in another form somewhere else because this would lead to confusion. Experience has abundantly proved that the representation of the broad typical sounds of English as provided for in Pitman's Shorthand is ample for all shorthand writers.

The pronunciation adopted in Pitman's Shorthand is based on that given in The New English Dictionary, edited by Sir James A. H. Murray, LL.D.

The shorthand alphabet consists of thin and thick strokes which represent the consonant sounds, and light and heavy dots and dashes which represent the vowel sounds. Thin strokes represent light sounds, thick strokes represent heavier sounds. Thin strokes are very thin, thick strokes are slightly firmer.

Any consonant symbol or combination of consonant symbols, with or without vowel signs, is known as an outline. Having written an outline correctly, a writer of Pitman 2000 Shorthand is able to recognize it and transcribe it without any hesitation.

The Consonants

With the exception of *w*, *y* and the aspirate *h*, the strokes representing the consonant sounds are derived from the simple geometrical structures shown in the following diagrams:

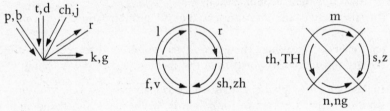

The following is an analysis of the diagrams:

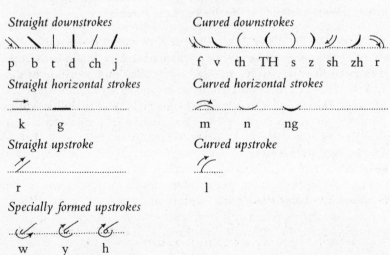

The Vowels

There are six *short* vowel sounds as heard in the sentence — and represented by light dots

ă ĕ ĭ ŏ ŭ ŏŏ
That pen is not much good.

and dashes

There are six *long* vowel sounds as heard in the sentence — and represented by heavy dots

ah ā ēe aw̄ ō ōō
Pā māy wē āll gō tōō?

and dashes

The vowel signs, i.e. dots and dashes, occupy three places against the consonant stroke as follows:

first place, where the stroke begins;
second place, in the middle of the stroke;
third place, at the end of the stroke.

The vowel places before and after strokes may be summarized as follows:

The vowel sounds which the signs represent are identified according to the place in which the dot or dash is written, e.g.:

a light dot at the beginning of a stroke represents the sound of ă as in 'at';
a light dot in the middle of a stroke represents the sound of ĕ as in 'said';
a heavy dot in the middle of a stroke represents the sound of ā as in 'day';
a heavy dot at the end of a stroke represents the sound of ē as in 'free';
and so on.

Outlines and their Positions

Any consonant sign or combination of consonant signs with or without vowel signs is referred to as an outline.

The first upstroke or downstroke in an outline is written either *above, on* or *through* the writing line according to the placement of the first vowel in the word, e.g.:

at   ă is a first-place vowel so the downstroke is written in first position, *above* the line;

aid   ā is a second-place vowel so the downstroke is written in second position, *on* the line;

eat   ē is a third-place vowel so the downstroke is written in third position, *through* the line;

law   aw is a first-place vowel so the upstroke is written in first position, *above* the line;

lay   ā is a second-place vowel so the upstroke is written in second position, *on* the line;

lee   ē is a third-place vowel so the upstroke is written in third position, *through* the line.

When writing shorthand the rules of position writing should be rigidly adhered to. After a short time this will become automatic. In this book every outline contains every sounded vowel until Unit 22, but when the theory has been thoroughly mastered, only essential vowels need to be written, and it will be the correct positioning of outlines, rather than vocalization, that will enable the outlines to be transcribed accurately and quickly. Therefore, all outlines, including short forms, must be written in their correct position from the very beginning of the learning of Pitman 2000 Shorthand.

Consonant R: Representation of some vowels

Many people do not pronounce **R** in words such as *far* and *door*. Therefore, it should be noted that the presence of **R** has a modifying effect upon a preceding vowel. Attention is therefore directed to the following observations with regard to the consonant **R**, to certain vowels when preceding **R** and to a class of vowels which may be described as more or less obscure.

(a) Wherever the consonant **R** occurs in the spelling of a word, in Pitman's Shorthand it must be represented as a consonant, either in upward form or in downward form, or as a hook.

(b) In words such as *bar, far, mar, tar, jar*, the first-place vowel-sign for **ah** is used; but in words such as *barrow, Farrow, marry* and *carry*, the first vowel-sound is to be represented by the first-place vowel-sign for **ă**.

(c) In words such as *four, fore, roar, lore, wore, shore, door, pour, core, gore, tore, sore*, the second-place vowel-sign for ō is used.

(d) In words such as *torch, morn, fork*, the first-place vowel-sign for ŏ is used.

(e) In words such as *air, fair, lair, bare*, the second-place vowel-sign for ā is used.

(f) In pairs of words such as *fir, fur; earth, worth; per, purr; Percy, pursy*; the vowel sound in the first word of the pair is represented by the second-place vowel-sign for ĕ; the vowel-sound in the second word of the pair is represented by the second-place vowel-sign for ŭ.

(g) In words such as *custody, custom, baron, felony, colour, factory, history*, the second vowel-sound is represented by the second-place vowel-sign for ŭ.

(h) In words such as *village, cottage, breakage*, the second vowel-sound is represented by the second-place vowel-sign for ĕ.

(i) In words such as *suppose*, the second vowel-sound is represented by the second-place vowel-sign for ō; but in words such as *supposition, disposition*, the second vowel-sound is represented by the second-place vowel-sign for ŭ.

The Aims of this Book are:

to present the complete theory of Pitman 2000 Shorthand in clear and easy stages;
to give adequate theory practice within a working vocabulary; and
to introduce transcription training and speed development.

Your Aims should be:

to understand thoroughly every shorthand rule in each unit and to follow the suggested practice plan;
to be able to read, write, recognize and visualize each outline without any hesitation; and
to read and write some shorthand every day.

How to Use this Book

Work through each unit thoroughly and conscientiously. No two students learn in exactly the same way or in the same amount of time and the practice plan may be adjusted to meet individual needs. It is essential to use the book in the order in which the units are presented and to learn and understand each shorthand rule before proceeding to the next unit.

Short Forms and Phrases

Short forms are the signs for some of the most frequently used words in the English language. It is most unlikely that any statement on a general business or industrial subject could be written in shorthand without using at least one short form, and therefore all short forms should be learned so thoroughly that they are written accurately in their correct position and without hesitation, and read back easily. Phrases in Pitman 2000 Shorthand are outlines formed together for groups of words which are used frequently, and the principles of phrasing must be understood so that they can be used whenever possible. Short forms and phrases are positive speed builders.

Reading Practice

The aim of every shorthand student is to write the spoken word at speed and to transcribe notes accurately and quickly. The development of the shorthand skill is positively aided when some part of every day is devoted to the reading of shorthand. Each exercise should be read thoroughly in preparation for copying and dictation practice. Any outline which causes hesitation in the first reading should be practised until it is completely familiar so that a second and third reading of any exercise can be read as quickly as longhand. The more you read, the better the visual image of the outlines becomes. When you write shorthand, you are writing as a result of recalling the specific shape of the outline. In addition to reading printed shorthand, time should be devoted each day to improving the speed of reading from your own notes. The whole purpose of taking shorthand notes is to be able to transcribe accurately and at speed. The monthly magazine *2000* provides excellent additional shorthand material for reading and copying practice.

Pen and Notebook

A pen is unquestionably the best writing implement because the 'thin' or 'thick' strokes produced by other writing implements are much less accurate and therefore more difficult to transcribe. The nib of the pen needs to be fine so that the necessary lightness of touch can be attained; it needs to be flexible so that it responds immediately to the slightest changes in pressure; it needs to be fluent so that it will move swiftly and smoothly over the paper, giving an even, continuous line.

The 'thin' or 'thick' strokes which are necessary for accurate transcription are only consistently possible when written with a carefully chosen shorthand pen. Ideally, one should try out several nibs until the necessary flexibility and fluency of line is attained because individual needs differ.

The cap should be removed from the pen and the pen should be held lightly between the index and second fingers of the writing hand with the thumb lying along the other side of the 'triangle' to give control. It should not be gripped tightly with tense fingers, but with only sufficient force for it to remain in the hand without sliding out. The fingers should be no more than slightly curved with the little finger only in contact with the writing surface. These may seem small, even insignificant, details but their importance in establishing good writing habits is very great.

Lined shorthand notebooks should be used for writing shorthand. The quality of the paper is a factor in helping you to write well; it should be smooth and well surfaced. Coarse paper will be too absorbent and will snag the writing implement and cause splutters. A good notebook should contain no more than about 80 leaves; it should be of the well-proved 5″ × 8″ (127 mm × 203 mm) size; it should be lined with about 21 lines to the page, at a line spacing of about 8 mm (3 lines to the inch), and preferably with a one-inch (25 mm) margin. If not printed, margins should be pencil-ruled in. It is necessary to have a margin on each page of your shorthand notebook so that when you are checking shorthand that you have written you can encircle any incorrect outline in your notes and write the correct outline in the margin. In the office the margin should be used to note any alterations and additions indicated by the dictator. All these dimensions have proved over the years to be the best. The line length is such that it involves only one slight hand shift. The thickness of the notebook when limited to not more than 80 leaves does not raise the hand too far for comfort above the surface of the table or desk. Write about eleven to fourteen outlines per line, and always write thick strokes lightly and thin strokes lighter still. This will help you to increase your speed in writing.

First Course Cassettes

After reading through and preparing each exercise, it is essential to practise writing it from dictation. As an aid to teachers, and to students who are teaching themselves Pitman 2000 Shorthand, specially prepared cassettes are available. The exercises and Short Form and Phrase Drills are dictated twice, Units 1–14 at 30 w.p.m. repeated at 50 w.p.m., followed by Units 15–25 dictated first at 40 w.p.m. then repeated at 50 w.p.m.

Shorthand notes should be checked against the printed outlines in the book, errors or omissions noted, and the correct outlines practised. The next time those words are dictated the outlines will be written correctly and without hesitation. Each rule should be thoroughly learned as it is introduced. Correct shorthand outlines are faster to write and easier to read. Attention should always be paid to the length of the strokes, the position of each outline in relation to the writing line, and the placing of the essential vowel signs.

Transcription

The importance of accurate and speedy transcription cannot be over-emphasized. Whenever possible a typed transcript should be made. It is helpful in the early stages of learning to type from the printed shorthand in this book, but when transcribing from your own notes you will find the printed shorthand invaluable as a key to your own notes. If you cannot read an outline in your notes check it against the printed version and make sure you understand why you could not read your own shorthand. Then write the outline several times.

Posture

Cultivating a good posture is important; not only does it suggest alertness and efficiency but it promotes a better writing style and actually prevents fatigue. Feet should be kept together firmly on the floor, the back well supported by the chair, and the weight of the upper part of the body on the non-writing arm.

Graded Material to First Course

Pitman 2000 Shorthand Dictation Practice and its complementary *Workbook, Parts 1 and 2* with the related cassettes should be introduced when Unit 5 of *First Course* has been completed. *Pitman 2000 Shorthand First Course Facility Drills* and *Graded Exercises* have been prepared on a unit-by-unit basis with *First Course*. In any skill, constant practice makes perfect, and by using these additional materials a greater efficiency will be achieved in a shorter time.

Speed

After a thorough preparation of each exercise, the aim should be to write it from dictation as fast as possible, bearing in mind that the reading speed of prepared material is higher than the present writing speed, but spare a thought for the one who will have to read your shorthand outlines. The answer is simple, it will be you. If your shorthand outlines are difficult to read take the trouble to improve them. It will be to your advantage to develop good writing habits from the beginning. After the completion of the study of Pitman 2000 Shorthand, followed by a course of revision and speed development, it will be possible to attain a writing speed of 140 w.p.m. You should be able to read shorthand at nearly twice this speed and transcribe on to the typewriter at 35 w.p.m.

Homework

Practising shorthand daily will ensure steady progress in the skill. A student of Pitman 2000 Shorthand should expect to spend some part of every day reading, practising outlines, learning short forms and phrasing principles and preparing the exercise material to be used the following day.

After First Course

On completion of this *First Course*, a good knowledge of Pitman 2000 Shorthand will have been attained. A complete theory revision and vocabulary extension is then necessary in preparation for a secretarial post. *Pitman 2000 Shorthand: First Course Review* provides a useful theory revision, with many additional examples of the rules of the system, a vocabulary range of five thousand words, and some concentrated revision material. *Pitman 2000 Shorthand: Phrase Book* is designed to increase the reading and writing skills in Pitman 2000 Shorthand by a full understanding of the phrasing principles which are explained and illustrated. Read all the Pitman 2000 Shorthand provided in *2000* magazine each month to complete a satisfactory programme of revision work.

Pitman 2000 Shorthand is designed for quick and therefore easy learning with a realistic speed potential to meet the demands of today's business world. A sound knowledge of the theory ensures that outlines can be written swiftly and the writer is able to transcribe them quickly and accurately into typewritten or handwritten form.

PERSONAL PREFACE
FOR STUDENTS
by Peter Pitman

Make sure you understand the theory. If you do not, do please ask your teacher to explain before moving on. Do develop readable outlines, for it is you yourself who will have to read them. Take time, particularly, to be sure of the vowels. Your problem will not be that your hand cannot move fast enough; it will be your brain which will not recall the visual image fast enough. So, read as much shorthand as you can, to become more familiar with many outlines.

Certain short forms will be used frequently, in fact, five words make up 18 per cent of continuous English, i.e., *the* 6 per cent, *of* 3·7 per cent, *to* 3·7 per cent, *and* 2·6 per cent, *in* 2·3 per cent. However, these are few and some apparently common words are quite infrequent, e.g., *remember* ·004 per cent, and *unfortunately* ·016 per cent.

You may be interested to know that this is the briefest form of recording on paper ever invented. I do hope you will enjoy your shorthand.

Table of Consonants

Unit	Character	Name	Letter(s)	As sounded in
1	⟍	pee	P	**p**aragra**p**h, ra**p**id
1	⟍	bee	B	**b**usiness, a**b**sence
1	|	tee	T	**t**ax, fa**t**e
1	|	dee	D	**d**epartment, excee**d**
2	—	kay	K	**c**alculator, lea**k**
2	—	gay	G	**g**ood, va**g**ue
2	⌒	em	M	**m**icrofil**m**, see**m**
2	⌣	en	N	**n**ote, see**n**
2	⌣	ing	NG	wro**ng**, puddi**ng**
3	⟍	ef	F	**f**uture, sa**f**e
3	⟍	vee	V	**v**alue, arri**v**e
3	(	ith	TH	**th**ank, clo**th**
3	(	thee	*TH*	**th**ese, brea**th**e
4	⌐ up	el	L	**l**ast, rea**l**
4	⟋ up	way	W	**w**ork, re**w**ard
4	⟍ up	yay	Y	**y**outh, law**y**er
5	⟋up ⟍down	ray, ar	R	**r**eceive, ti**r**e
7	⟋	chay	CH	**ch**eque/**ch**eck, ri**ch**
7	⟋	jay	J	**j**ustice, e**dg**e
7	⟋	ish	SH	**sh**orthand, da**sh**
7&13	)	ess	S	i**ce**, me**ss**y
13	)	zee	Z	**z**ero, co**s**y
15	⟋	zhee	ZH	u**s**ual, mira**g**e
15	⟋ up	hay	H	**h**yphen, per**h**aps

UNIT 1

P, B, T, D
Vowels Ā and Ō
Circle S

P is a thin stroke written *downwards* ⟍ .
Vowel **Ā** is a heavy dot. It is always written at the middle of a stroke, and is always added after the writing of the outline has been completed. In the word *pay* the vowel is sounded *after* the **P** and is placed *after* the

stroke **P** ⟍ *pay* (on the right-hand side).
In the word *ape* the vowel **Ā** is sounded *before* the **P** and is placed *before*

the stroke **P** ⟍ *ape* (on the left-hand side) *after* the stroke has been written.

B is a thick stroke written *downwards* ⟍ .
Vowel **Ō** is a heavy dash. It is always written at the middle of a stroke, and is added *after* the writing of the outline has been completed. In the word *oboe* the vowels are sounded *before* and *after* the **B** and are placed

before and *after* the stroke **B** ⟍ *oboe* (on the left- and right-hand sides). The **Ā** and **Ō** vowels are known as second-place vowels.

T is a thin stroke written *downwards* ⏐ . In the words *toe/tow* the

vowel is sounded *after* the **T** and is placed *after* the stroke **T** ⏐ *toe/tow* (on the right-hand side).

D is a thick stroke written *downwards* ⏐ . A small circle written as shown at the *end* of the stroke in an anti-clockwise direction adds the

sound of **S** or **Z** ⏐ . In the words *days/daze* the vowel is sounded

after the **D** and is placed *after* the stroke **D** ⏐ *days/daze* (on the right-hand side). The **circle S** or **Z** at the end of an outline is always read last.

1

Unit 1

The sound of **S** at the beginning of a word is shown by a small circle written on the right-hand side of straight downstrokes in an anti-clockwise direction:

.... *soap* (sounded first)

.... *days/daze* (sounded last)

.... *soaps* (sounded first and last)

The **circle S** at the beginning of an outline is always read first.

Always complete the writing of outlines *before* adding the vowels.

Position Writing

In the following examples all the single downstrokes are uniform in length and are written to the line. These are known as second-position outlines.

pays/pace base/bays space stow stows stay stays oats aid aids day

Practise writing these outlines in your notebook. Write each outline several times, repeating the words out loud as you write.

When two or more strokes are joined together the first stroke is written to the line and the outline is completed without lifting the pen.

Complete the strokes as in ....; then write in the vowel .... *boat.*

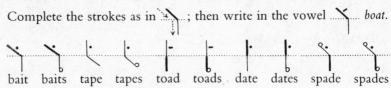

bait baits tape tapes toad toads date dates spade spades

Write each outline several times, repeating the word aloud as you write. Make sure that all of the strokes are uniform in length.

Short Forms

Certain words are used so frequently in the English language that special signs called **short forms** are used to represent them, and it is necessary to memorize them. Three positions are used for the writing of short forms. Some short forms are written above the line (first position); some are written on the line (second position); and some are written through the line (third position). The writing of all outlines in their correct positions is most important as this will enable the outlines to be transcribed accurately and quickly.

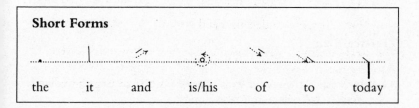

the	it	and	is/his	of	to	today

Practise these short forms until they are completely familiar and can be written and transcribed without hesitation.

Phrases

The outlines for two or more words may be joined without lifting the pen, to make outlines called **phrases**. Good phrasing leads to high-speed writing. Phrasing is used, however, only when outlines join naturally and can be read back easily.

In a phrase the word *the* is represented by a tick joined to the stroke it follows. This tick is written upwards or downwards to form a sharp angle. After **P** and **B** it is written down to the left ; after **T** and **D** it is written up to the right . After final **circle S** attached to a straight stroke the **tick the** is written down to the left .

The first outline in a phrase is written in its usual position.

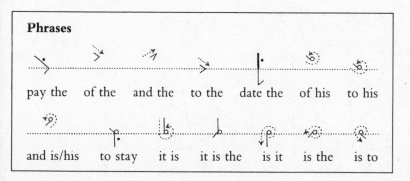

pay the	of the	and the	to the	date the	of his	to his
and is/his	to stay	it is	it is the	is it	is the	is to

Unit 1

Punctuation, etc.

This is the same in shorthand as in longhand except for:

full stop ⠐⠭ question mark ⠦ exclamation mark ⠖

dash ⠤ hyphen ⠢ parentheses ⠶

Practice Plan

1 Read through the exercise.
2 Practise writing any outline which caused any hesitancy in the reading. Say the word to yourself as you write.
3 Read through the exercise again, aiming for fluency in your reading.
4 Copy each sentence until you can write it easily and rapidly.
5 Write each sentence from dictation. Keep your book open for reference if necessary.
6 Close the textbook. Read the sentences from your own shorthand notes.
7 Encircle any incorrect outline and write the correct outline in the margin.

Exercise 1

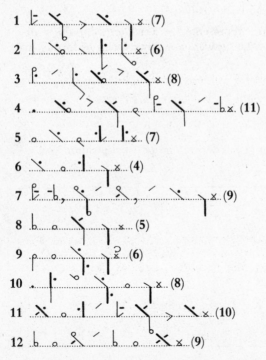

4

K, G, M, N, NG
Dot ING

The strokes for **K, G, M, N** and **NG** are horizontal, uniform in size, and are written from *left to right*:

K (thin) ......➤ **G** (thick) ......➤ **M** (thin and curved) ......

N (thin and curved) ...... **NG** (thick and curved) ......

When a vowel is sounded first it is written *above* those strokes, and written *below* when it is sounded after. Always write the stroke first.

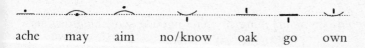

ache   may   aim   no/know   oak   go   own

Always write the **circle S** on top of straight horizontal strokes (anti-clockwise) and inside horizontal curved strokes:

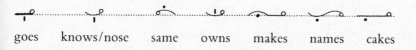

goes   knows/nose   same   owns   makes   names   cakes

Read the outlines and then copy them several times.

In the above examples the horizontal strokes are written on the line (in second position). When horizontal strokes are combined with other strokes the first downstroke is written to the line:

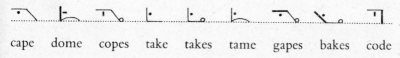

cape   dome   copes   take   takes   tame   gapes   bakes   code

Unit 2

Dot ING

A dot at the end of the last stroke of an outline represents the suffix **ING**. Write the stroke or strokes first, then the **dot ING**, and the vowel sign last.

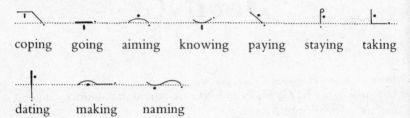

coping   going   aiming   knowing   paying   staying   taking

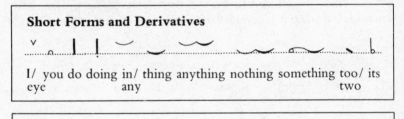

dating   making   naming

Read the above outlines and then copy them several times.

Derivative is the term used for a word built from another word called the root word. For example, *any* is a root word, *anything* is a derivative.

Short Forms and Derivatives

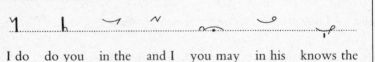

I/ you do doing in/ thing anything nothing something too/ its
eye   any   two

Phrases

Tick the is written downward to the left after **K, G, N, NG** and **circle S** attached to these strokes.

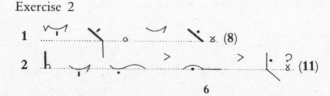

I do   do you   in the   and I   you may   in his   knows the

---

Read the practice plan on page 4 *before* you begin work on Exercise 2.

Exercise 2

1 ....⌐⌐.........⌐⌐.........⌐.........⌐⌐ x. **(8)**

2 .ɭ........⌐⌐...........⌐......... > ......⌐......... > .⌐. ? x. **(11)**

6

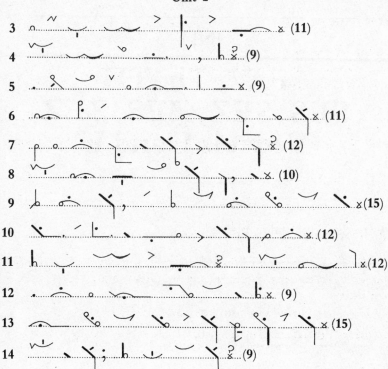

UNIT 3

F, V, Th, TH
SES, SEZ, ZES, ZEZ
Vowels Ĕ and Ŭ

F is a thin, curved downstroke ......:

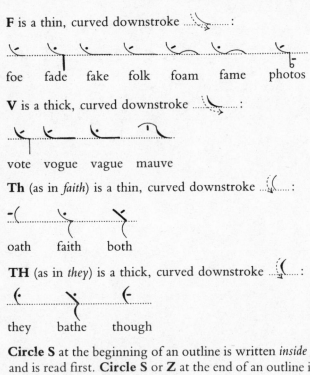

foe fade fake folk foam fame photos

V is a thick, curved downstroke ......:

vote vogue vague mauve

Th (as in *faith*) is a thin, curved downstroke ......:

oath faith both

TH (as in *they*) is a thick, curved downstroke ......:

they bathe though

Circle S at the beginning of an outline is written *inside* curved strokes and is read first. **Circle S** or **Z** at the end of an outline is written *inside* curved strokes and is read last:

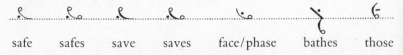

safe safes save saves face/phase bathes those

Read the outlines and then practise writing them several times. Make sure the strokes are uniform in length.

8

The sound of **SES**, **SEZ**, **ZES** or **ZEZ** at the end of a word is represented by a large circle written at the end of an outline and is read last. Make sure this **SES** circle is written larger than the **circle S**:

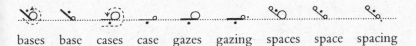

bases   basc   cases   case   gazes   gazing   spaces   space   spacing

The **SES**, **SEZ**, **ZES** and **ZEZ** circles written at the end of an outline are *always* written inside curved strokes and are read last:

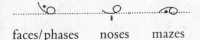

faces/phases   noses   mazes

Read the above outlines and write them several times. Then read the following sentences, copy them and write them several times from dictation.

Exercise 3

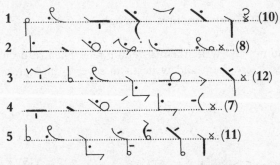

1 .... **(10)**

2 .... **(8)**

3 .... **(12)**

4 .... **(7)**

5 .... **(11)**

The short sound Ĕ (as in *bet*) is represented by a light dot which is always written at the middle of a stroke (in second place), either before or after it, wherever it is sounded:

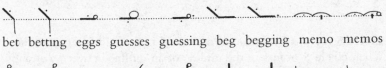

bet   betting   eggs   guesses   guessing   beg   begging   memo   memos

sets   setting   sense   them   said   debt   debts   effect   effects

Read the above outlines and write them several times. Then read the following sentences, copy them and write them several times from dictation.

Exercise 4

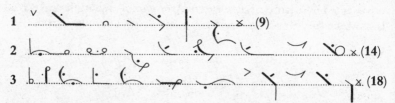

The short sound Ŭ (as in *up*) is represented by a light dash which is always placed at the middle of a stroke (in second place), either before or after it, wherever it is sounded. Remember that when an outline begins with a horizontal stroke and is followed by a down-stroke, it is the downstroke which *positions* the outline:

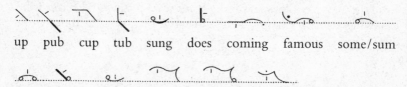

up   pub   cup   tub   sung   does   coming   famous   some/sum

sums   bus   sun/son   month   months   enough

Read the above outlines and write them several times. Then read the following sentences, copy them and write them several times from dictation.

Exercise 5

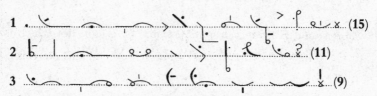

Circle S represents the sound of **S** or **Z** in the middle of an outline. When **circle S** occurs in the middle of an outline between a straight horizontal stroke and a straight downstroke, or a straight downstroke and a straight horizontal stroke, it is always written *outside* the angle made by the two straight strokes:

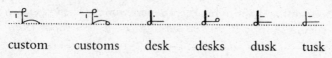

custom   customs   desk   desks   dusk   tusk

When **circle S** occurs in the *middle* of an outline between two curved strokes it is written *inside* the first curve, and *inside* the curved stroke when it occurs between a straight stroke and a curved stroke, or a curved stroke and a straight stroke:

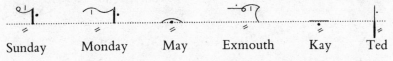

unsafe	mason	dozen	unsaid	musk

Two light dashes (written *upwards*) under an outline indicate a word requiring an initial capital letter:

Sunday	Monday	May	Exmouth	Kay	Ted

Read the outlines and then copy them several times.

Short Forms and Derivatives

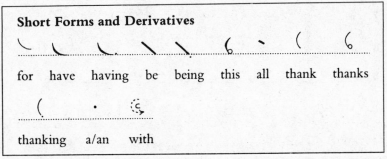

for	have	having	be	being	this	all	thank	thanks

thanking	a/an	with

Phrases

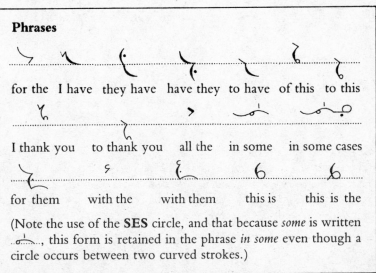

for the	I have	they have	have they	to have	of this	to this

I thank you	to thank you	all the	in some	in some cases

for them	with the	with them	this is	this is the

(Note the use of the **SES** circle, and that because *some* is written ⌐⌐⌐, this form is retained in the phrase *in some* even though a circle occurs between two curved strokes.)

Unit 3

Read the practice plan on page 4 *before* you begin work on Exercise 6.

Exercise 6

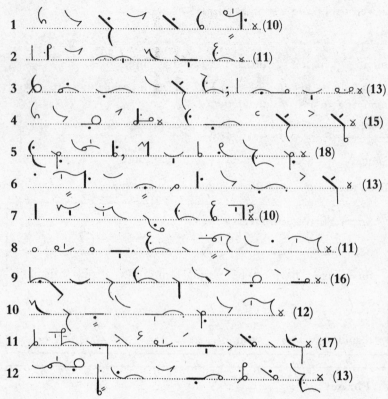

L, W, Y
Past-tense sounds T, D or ED

L is a thin curved upstroke ⟋ :

low loading lay lays laying else sail/sale sailing bowl scale

envelope slow mail/male slope delays sold told legs luck length

old fail lungs developing muscle

Read the **circle S** first, in the middle, or last, wherever it is written. Between **L** and **N** write **circle S** inside the **L** and complete the circle before writing the **N**:

lesson lessons

The **circle S** is not completed after a downward curve or **N** followed by **L**. The circle is written to the curved stroke but the following **L** comes *out of the circle* as shown in the following outlines:

vessel nestle senseless

Read the above outlines and copy them several times. Then read the following sentences, copy them and write them several times from dictation.

Exercise 7

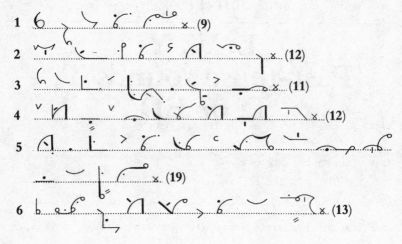

1 (9)
2 (12)
3 (11)
4 (12)
5 (19)
6 (13)

W is a thin straight upstroke with a small hook at the beginning :

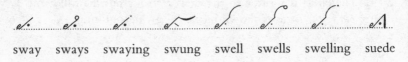

way/weigh   weighing   welcome   weld   Wednesday   twelve

well   unwell   wake   wakes   web   wedding

A small **circle S** is written inside the hook of **W** to represent the sound of **SW** :

sway   sways   swaying   swung   swell   swells   swelling   suede

Read the above outlines and then copy them several times.

The sound added to most weak verbs to make a past tense is that of a **T, D** or **ED**. These past tenses are shown by writing a disjoined

14

stroke **T** or **D** (according to whichever is sounded) close to the root outline. The disjoined **T** or **D** is also used for some adjectives where applicable:

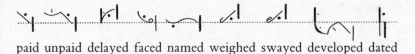

paid unpaid delayed faced named weighed swayed developed dated

Read the outlines and then write them several times.

Y is a thin straight upstroke with a small hook at the beginning :

yellow   young   yolk/yoke   yes   yell   yelling

Read the above outlines and write them several times. Then read the following sentences, copy them and write them several times from dictation.

Exercise 8

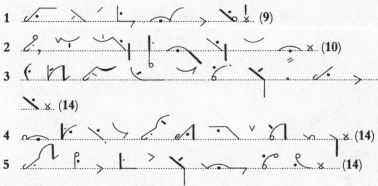

1   (9)

2   (10)

3   (14)

4   (14)

5   (14)

Short Forms and Derivatives

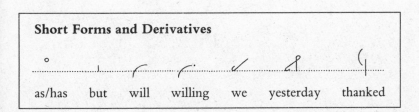

as/has   but   will   willing   we   yesterday   thanked

15

Unit 4

Phrases

In phrasing, use only the first half of the short form **I** before the stroke **L**.

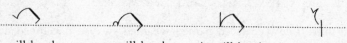

I will be the   you will be the   it will be the   I thanked

they will be   you will have the   but the   but you will be the

we have the   as we have the   we will be   and as/has

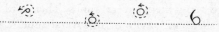

as/has the   is as   as is   this has

Note that the outline for *but the* is tilted to the right to give a better angle.

To form a phrase, **tick the** can be added to a disjoined **T** or **D**.

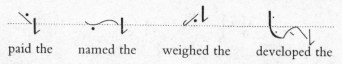

paid the   named the   weighed the   developed the

Read the practice plan on page 4 *before* you begin work on Exercise 9.

Exercise 9

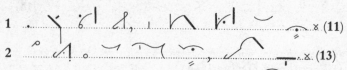

1 ... **(11)**
2 ... **(13)**
3 ... **(11)**
4 ... **(12)**
5 ... **(13)**

16

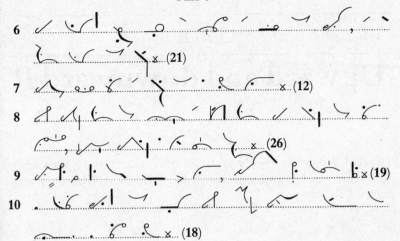

UNIT 5

Upward and downward R

Upward **R** is a thin straight upstroke written ⟍ and is used when the sound of **R** begins a word. Write circles **S** or **SES** on top of upward **R**:

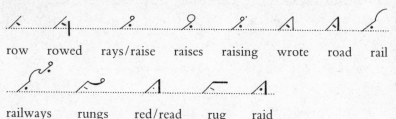

row   rowed   rays/raise   raises   raising   wrote   road   rail

railways   rungs   red/read   rug   raid

Upward **R** is used in the *middle* of an outline:

purpose forth board work worked world girls word Thursday

Upward **R** is used at the end of an outline when the **R** is followed by a sounded vowel:

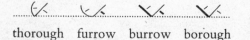

thorough   furrow   burrow   borough

Read the above outlines and write them several times. Then read the following sentences, copy them and write them several times from dictation.

Exercise 10

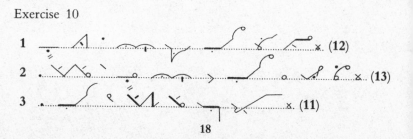

1 .... x. (12)

2 .... x. (13)

3 .... x. (11)

18

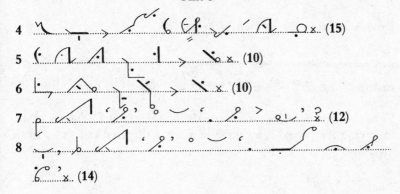

4   **(15)**

5   **(10)**

6   **(10)**

7   **(12)**

8   **(14)**

Downward **R** is a thin curved downstroke .... and is used when a vowel sound *begins* a word and **R** is the first consonant sound:

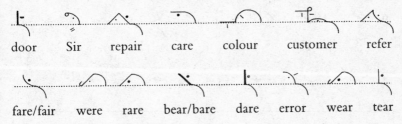

air/heir   airs   airing   oars   earth   erase   airless

Downward **R** is used when the sound of **R** *ends* a word:

door   Sir   repair   care   colour   customer   refer

fare/fair   were   rare   bear/bare   dare   error   wear   tear

Downward **R** is retained in derivatives when downward **R** is used in the root outline:

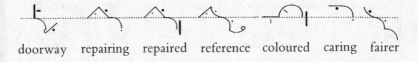

doorway   repairing   repaired   reference   coloured   caring   fairer

Downward **R** is used when immediately followed by **circle S** or **SES** circle:

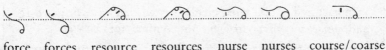

force   forces   resource   resources   nurse   nurses   course/coarse

Downward **R** is *always* used before **M**:

roam   Rome   term   firm   firms   rum   forum

Read the above outlines and write them several times. Then read the following sentences, copy them and write them several times from dictation.

Exercise 11

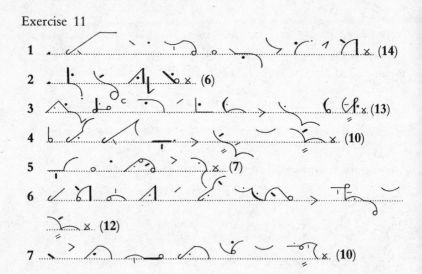

1 ... (14)

2 ... (6)

3 ... (13)

4 ... (10)

5 ... (7)

6 ... (12)

7 ... (10)

Short Forms and Derivatives

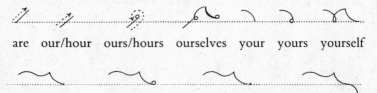

are   our/hour   ours/hours   ourselves   your   yours   yourself

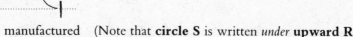

manufacture   manufactures   manufacturing   manufacturer

manufactured   (Note that **circle S** is written *under* **upward R** and *inside* the first curve in the outline for *ourselves*.)

Phrases

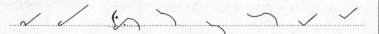

you are   we are   they were   of your   to your   in your   to our   of our

In phrases **circle S** is used for *us* and *his*:

to us   for us   of us   with us   to his   for his   of his   with his

In some phrases the short form for the word *you* is turned sideways to give an easier joining:

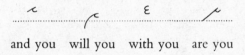

and you   will you   with you   are you

Read the practice plan on page 4 *before* you begin work on Exercise 12.

Exercise 12

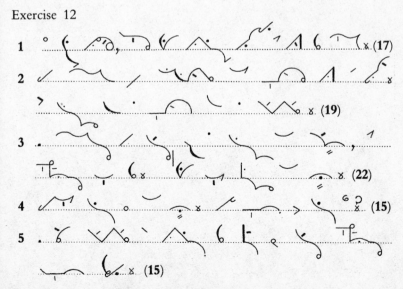

Unit 5

6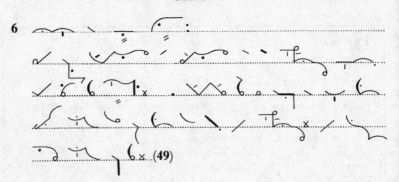

(49)

Short Form and Phrase Drill

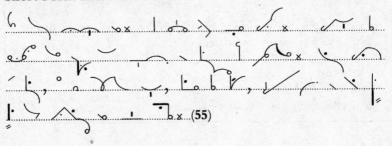

(55)

UNIT 6

Half-length strokes

In one-syllable words thin strokes are halved in length to indicate the following sound of **T** and **circle S** may be added to the half-length stroke:

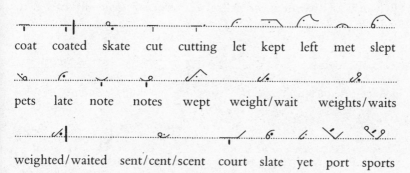

| coat | coated | skate | cut | cutting | let | kept | left | met | slept |

| pets | late | note | notes | wept | weight/wait | weights/waits |

| weighted/waited | sent/cent/scent | court | slate | yet | port | sports |

Read the outlines and then write them several times.

In one-syllable words thick strokes are halved in length to indicate the following sound of **D** and **circle S** may be added to the half-length stroke:

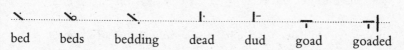

| bed | beds | bedding | dead | dud | goad | goaded |

Read the above outlines and write them several times. Then read the following sentences, copy them and write them several times from dictation.

Exercise 13

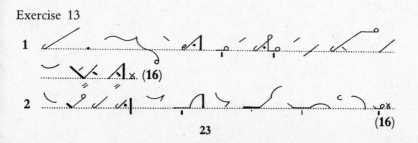

1 .... (16)

2 .... (16)

23

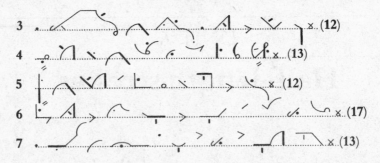

3 .... (12)
4 .... (13)
5 .... (12)
6 .... (17)
7 .... (13)

In words of two or more syllables a stroke is generally halved to indicate a following sound of **T** or **D**:

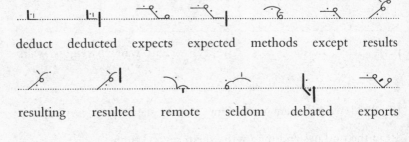

deduct   deducted   expects   expected   methods   except   results

resulting   resulted   remote   seldom   debated   exports

support   report

Read the outlines and then write them several times.

Strokes are *not* halved if the halving would not clearly show:

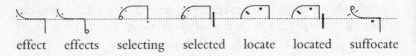

effect   effects   selecting   selected   locate   located   suffocate

Half-length upward **R** is never written standing alone or with just a final circle; it would be much too easy to confuse it with other outlines:

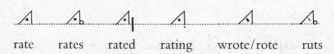

rate   rates   rated   rating   wrote/rote   ruts

24

The strokes for **R** and **L** are not halved for **D** when a sounded vowel comes between **R-D**, **L-D**:

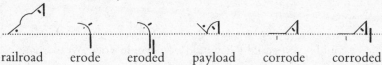

railroad   erode   eroded   payload   corrode   corroded

Read the above outlines and write them several times. Then read the following sentences, copy them and write them several times from dictation.

Exercise 14

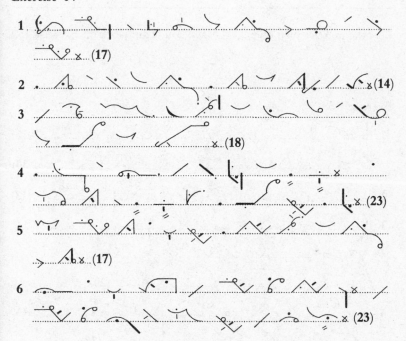

1 .... (17)

2 .... (14)

3 .... (18)

4 .... (23)

5 .... (17)

6 .... (23)

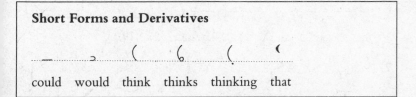

Short Forms and Derivatives

could   would   think   thinks   thinking   that

Phrases

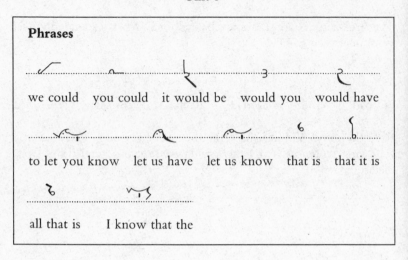

we could   you could   it would be   would you   would have

to let you know   let us have   let us know   that is   that it is

all that is   I know that the

Read the practice plan on page 4 *before* you begin work on Exercise 15.

Exercise 15

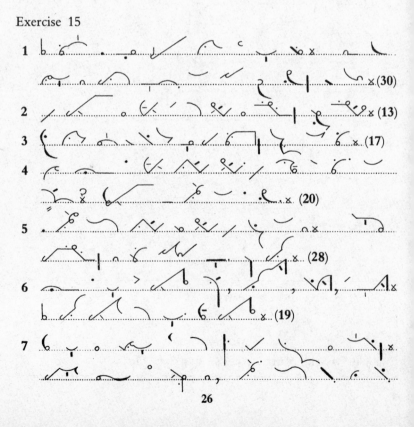

Unit 6

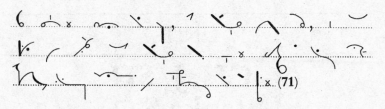

Short Form and Phrase Drill

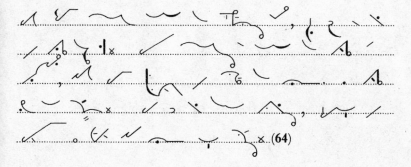

UNIT 7

CH, J, SH
Stroke S (1)

CH is a thin downstroke ....../....... :

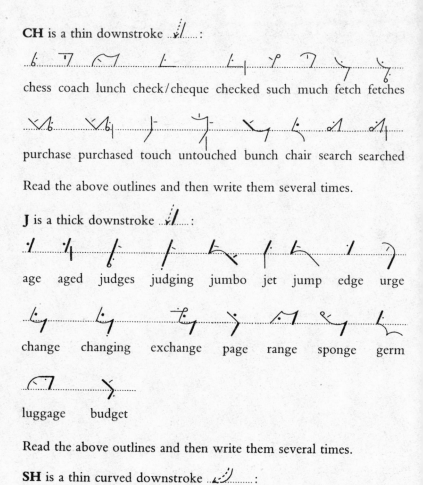

chess coach lunch check/cheque checked such much fetch fetches

purchase purchased touch untouched bunch chair search searched

Read the above outlines and then write them several times.

J is a thick downstroke ....../....... :

age aged judges judging jumbo jet jump edge urge

change changing exchange page range sponge germ

luggage budget

Read the above outlines and then write them several times.

SH is a thin curved downstroke ....../....... :

show showing shade shades shame shape shaping share

28

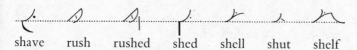

| shave | rush | rushed | shed | shell | shut | shelf |

Read the above outlines and write them several times. Then read the following sentences, copy them and write them several times from dictation.

Exercise 16

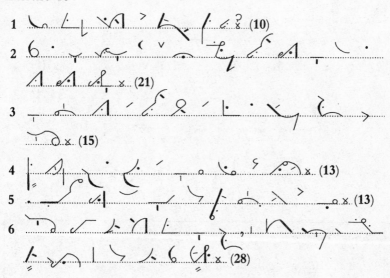

S is a thin curved downstroke 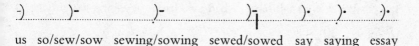 . When S is the only consonant sound in a word stroke S is used:

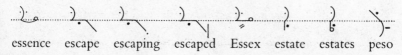

| us | so/sew/sow | sewing/sowing | sewed/sowed | say | saying | essay |

Stroke S is also used when a vowel is sounded *before* S at the beginning of a word, and when a vowel *follows* S at the end of a word:

| essence | escape | escaping | escaped | Essex | estate | estates | peso |

Unit 7

S–vowel–S or S–vowel–Z at the beginning of an outline is represented by **stroke S** followed by **circle S**:

says   sews/sows   Sussex   suspect   suspected

Read the above outlines and write them several times. Then read the following sentences, copy them and write them several times from dictation.

Exercise 17

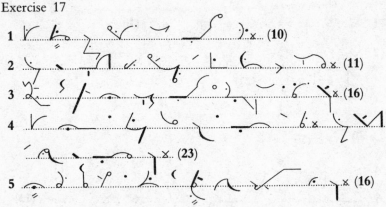

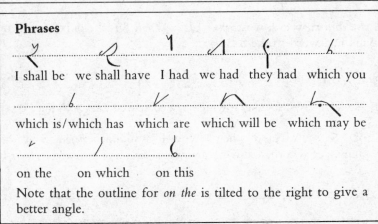

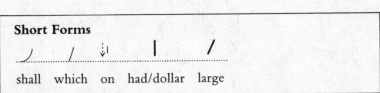

Short Forms

shall   which   on   had/dollar   large

Phrases

I shall be   we shall have   I had   we had   they had   which you

which is/which has   which are   which will be   which may be

on the   on which   on this

Note that the outline for *on the* is tilted to the right to give a better angle.

30

Unit 7

Read the practice plan on page 4 *before* you begin work on Exercise 18.

Exercise 18

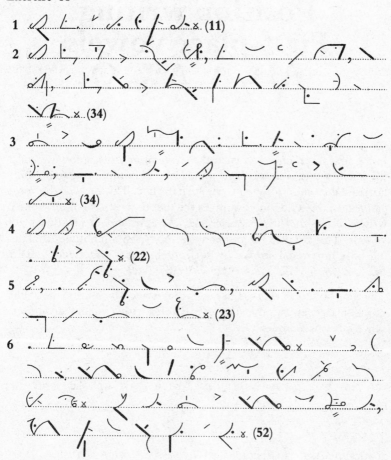

Short Form and Phrase Drill

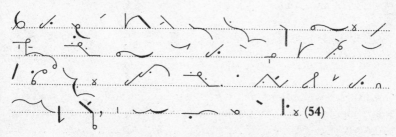

UNIT 8

Position writing
First-place vowels
AH, Ă, AW, Ŏ

In the first seven units, downstrokes have been written downwards *to* the line, upstrokes upwards *from* the line and outlines containing only horizontal strokes from left to right *on* the line. This is called the *second position*. In the following examples the first downstroke or upstroke is written *above* the line because **AH, Ă, AW** and **Ŏ** are first-place vowels. This is called the *first position*. First-position outlines containing only horizontal strokes or horizontal strokes and **circle S, SES, SEZ, ZES** or **ZEZ** are written *above* the line.

The long sound of **AH** (as in *car*) is represented by a heavy dot. This dot is placed at the *beginning* of a stroke, either before or after it, wherever it is sounded:

car arm part parting art guard March dark arch far farm cart

mark market marketing pass passed calm charges laugh

Remember that the *first* vowel sound in a word determines the position of an outline:

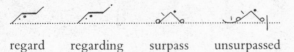

regard regarding surpass unsurpassed

Read the above outlines and write them several times. Then read the following sentences, copy them and write them several times from dictation.

Exercise 19

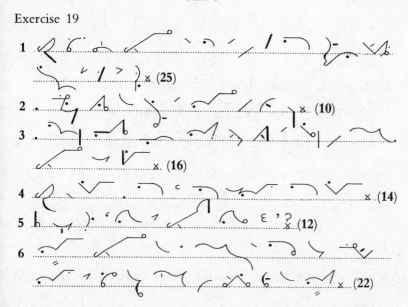

The short sound of **Ă** (as in *bag*) is represented by a light dot. This dot is placed at the *beginning* of a stroke, either before or after it, wherever it is sounded. When the first sounded vowel in a word is a first-place vowel the first downstroke or upstroke is written above the line:

bag   salad   added   attack   arrange   acted   match   cashed   away

manage   parade

fact   Saturday   adapt   manage   parade   attach   masses   catch   afford

balance   bad   bank   attempt   at

Read the above outlines and write them several times. Then read the following sentences and write them several times from dictation.

Exercise 20

1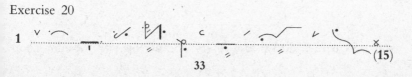

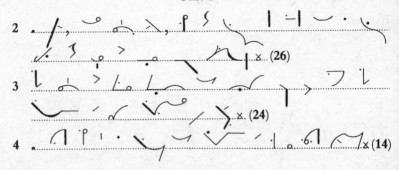

2

3

4

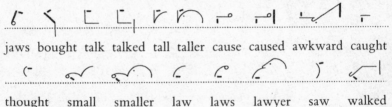

The sound of **AW** (as in *jaw*) is represented by a heavy dash written at the *beginning* of a stroke, either before or after it, wherever it is sounded. When the first sounded vowel in a word is a first-place vowel the first downstroke or upstroke is written above the line:

jaws   bought   talk   talked   tall   taller   cause   caused   awkward   caught

thought   small   smaller   law   laws   lawyer   saw   walked

Read the above outlines and write them several times. Then read the following sentences, copy them and write them several times from dictation.

Exercise 21

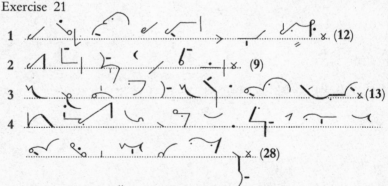

1

2

3

4

The short sound of **Ŏ** (as in *top*) is represented by a light dash. This dash is placed at the *beginning* of a stroke, either before or after it, wherever it is sounded:

top   odd   corner   docks   loss   losses   not   off   operate   jobs   lot   shop

form   formal   watches   got   wrong   was   or   song   long   oppose

because   bottom   short

Remember that it is the first vowel sound in a word which determines the position of an outline.

Read the above outlines and write them several times. Then read the following sentences, copy them and write them several times from dictation.

Exercise 22

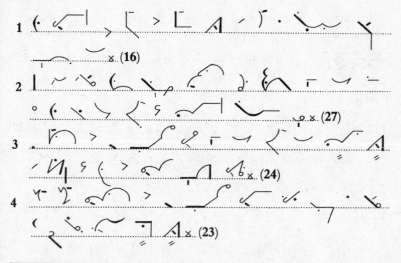

Short Forms and Derivatives

ought   owe/oh   owes   owing   owed   always   also   although

tomorrow

35

Phrases

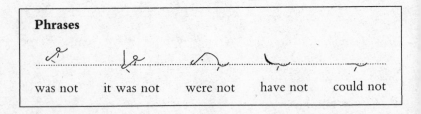

| was not | it was not | were not | have not | could not |

Intersections

A single stroke may be written through another stroke to represent a frequently occurring word. When convenient stroke **CH** may be intersected for the word *charge*, and stroke **F** for the word *form*:

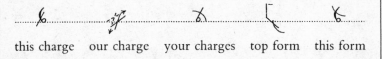

| this charge | our charge | your charges | top form | this form |

Read the practice plan on page 4 *before* you begin work on Exercise 23.

Exercise 23

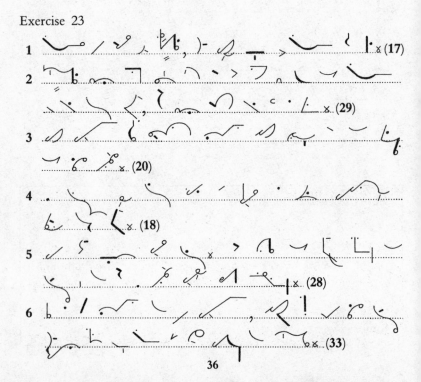

1 ... (17)

2 ... (29)

3 ... (20)

4 ... (18)

5 ... (28)

6 ... (33)

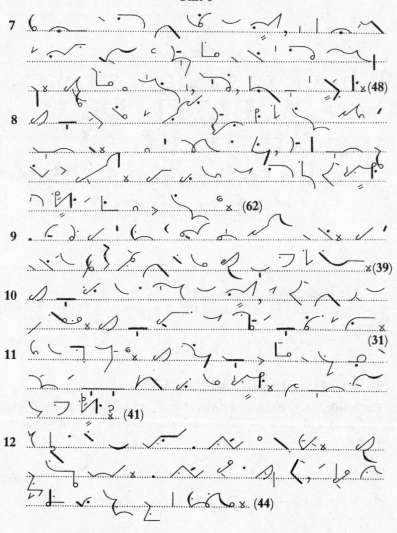

7 ... (48)

8 ... (62)

9 ... (39)

10 ... (31)

11 ... (41)

12 ... (44)

Short Form and Phrase Drill

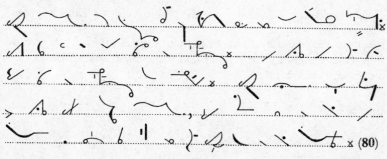

... (80)

L hook to straight strokes: PL, BL, TL, DL CHL, JL, KL, GL Circles to hooked strokes Suffix -ings

A small hook at the beginning of a straight downstroke and the horizontals **K** and **G**, written on the same side as the **circle S**, adds the sound of **L**.

PL BL TL DL CHL JL KL GL

The **hook L** is used *consonantally*, that is, the two consonants follow each other with no vowel between them. Write the hook first then the stroke:

play playing plates pleasant planet blades blanket claim

class enclosing glazing glaring glut clock cleanser clerk

Read the above outlines and write them several times. Then read the following sentences, copy them and write them several times from dictation.

Exercise 24

1 .... (14)

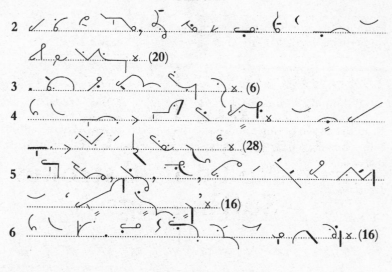

2 ... (20)

3 ... x. (6)

4 ... x ... (28)

5 ... x... (16)

6 ... x. (16)

The **hook L** is also used *syllabically*:

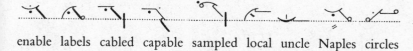

enable labels cabled capable sampled local uncle Naples circles

Read the above outlines and write them several times. Then read the following sentences, copy them and write them several times from dictation.

Exercise 25

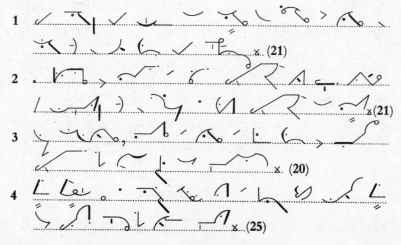

1 ... x. (21)

2 ... x(21)

3 ... x. (20)

4 ... x. (25)

Unit 9

Outlines for words that end with the sound of **TL** or **DL**, however this syllable is spelled, are always written with **hook L**:

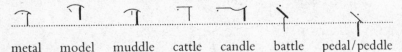

metal   model   muddle   cattle   candle   battle   pedal/peddle

Read the above outlines and write them several times. Then read the following sentences, copy them and write them several times from dictation.

Exercise 26

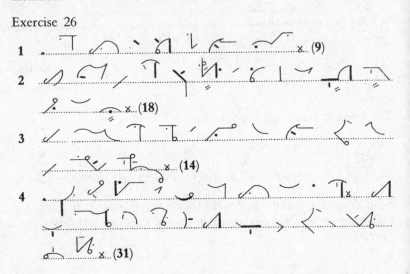

The sound of **S** is added to the **hook L** by writing the **circle S** inside the hook, at the beginning or in the middle of an outline.

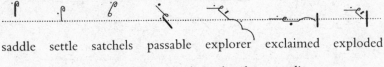

saddle   settle   satchels   passable   explorer   exclaimed   exploded

Note the positioning of the vowels in the above outlines.

A small dash written at the end of an outline represents the suffix **INGS**:

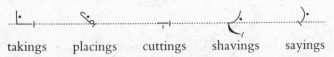

takings   placings   cuttings   shavings   sayings

Read the above outlines and write them several times.

Unit 9

Always practise the short forms and phrases. Make sure you write them in their correct positions.

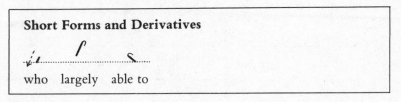

Short Forms and Derivatives

who   largely   able to

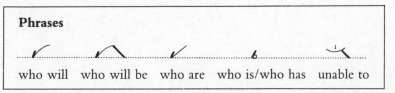

Phrases

who will   who will be   who are   who is/who has   unable to

Read the practice plan on page 4 *before* you begin work on Exercise 27.

Exercise 27

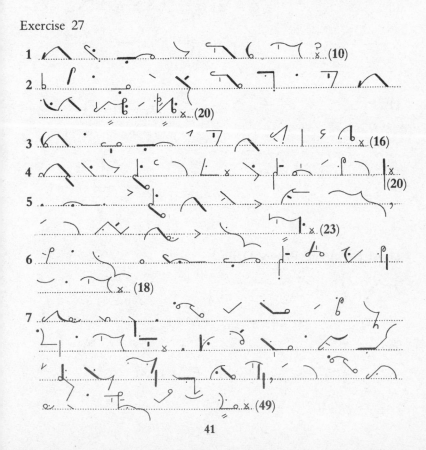

41

Unit 9

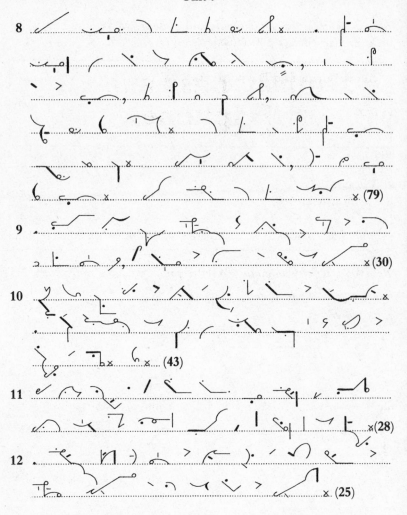

8   (79)

9   (30)

10   (43)

11   (28)

12   (25)

Short Form and Phrase Drill

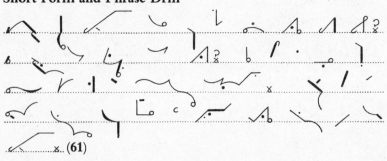

(61)

UNIT 10

Diphthongs I and OI Triphones

A diphthong is two vowel sounds pronounced as one. The diphthong **I** (as in *by*) is represented by the sign ....^v.... written at the beginning, in the middle or at the end of an outline, wherever it is sounded. The sign for **I** is generally written in *first place*. When the **I** diphthong is the first sounded vowel in a word the outline is written in first position:

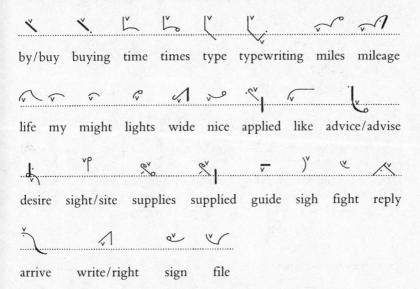

| by/buy | buying | time | times | type | typewriting | miles | mileage |

| life | my | might | lights | wide | nice | applied | like | advice/advise |

| desire | sight/site | supplies | supplied | guide | sigh | fight | reply |

| arrive | write/right | sign | file |

The large circle representing **SES, SEZ, ZES** or **ZEZ** may be used in the middle and at the end of an outline. When any vowel other than ĕ occurs between the two consonants, the vowel is inserted in the circle. **Circle S** can be added to the large circle:

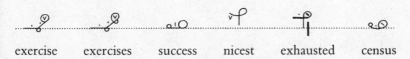

| exercise | exercises | success | nicest | exhausted | census |

43

Unit 10

The sign for **I** is joined to a stroke at the *beginning* of an outline when it immediately precedes a downstroke, and is joined to stroke **N** at the *end* of an outline:

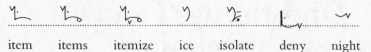

item   items   itemize   ice   isolate   deny   night

Read the above outlines and write them several times. Then read the following sentences and write them several times from dictation.

Exercise 28

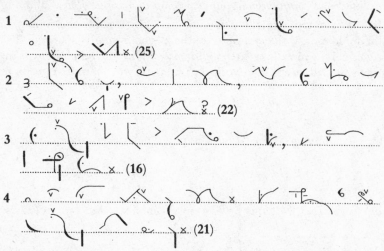

1 ... (25)

2 ... (22)

3 ... (16)

4 ... (21)

The diphthong **OI** (as in *boy*) is represented by the sign 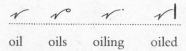 written at the beginning, in the middle or at the end of an outline, wherever it is sounded. The sign for **OI** is written in *first place*:

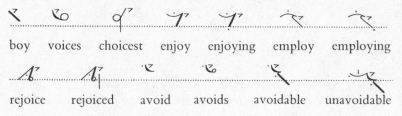

boy   voices   choicest   enjoy   enjoying   employ   employing

rejoice   rejoiced   avoid   avoids   avoidable   unavoidable

When **OI** precedes **L** at the beginning of a word, the sign for **OI** is joined:

oil   oils   oiling   oiled

44

Unit 10

A small tick added to the diphthongs **I** and **OI** indicates any following vowel sound and the sign is called a **triphone**:

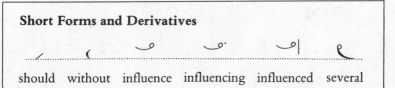

buyer   via   science   employee   voyage   dial   royal   enjoyable

Read the above outlines and then write them several times.

Short Forms and Derivatives

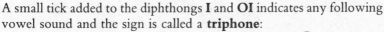

should   without   influence   influencing   influenced   several

---

Phrases

The first half of the sign for **I** is joined at the beginning of a phrase before **K, G, M, W,** upward **L,** upward **R** or a hooked downstroke:

I came   I expect   I go   I am   I may   I was   I will   I wrote   I play

Halving is used in conjunction with stroke **M** to represent the word *time* in phrases:

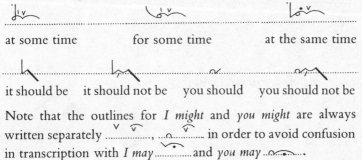

at some time   for some time   at the same time

it should be   it should not be   you should   you should not be

Note that the outlines for *I might* and *you might* are always written separately ...., ... in order to avoid confusion in transcription with *I may*............and *you may*.............

Exercise 29

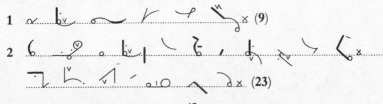

1 .... (9)

2 .... (23)

45

Unit 10

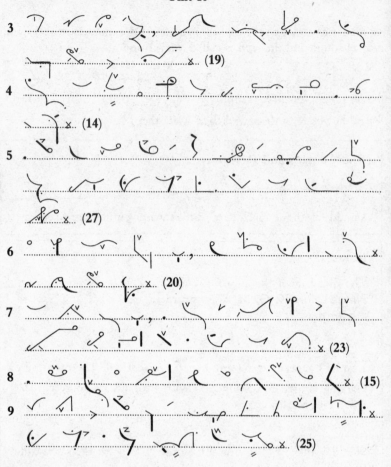

3 .... (19)

4 .... (14)

5 .... (27)

6 .... (20)

7 .... (23)

8 .... (15)

9 .... (25)

Short Form and Phrase Drill

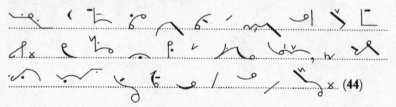

.... (44)

Loops ST and STER MD, ND

A shallow loop, half the length of the stroke to which it is attached, represents the sound of **ST**. It may be written at the beginning, in the middle, or at the end of an outline *unless* the outline begins or ends with a vowel. The **ST loop** is written in the same direction as **circle S** and is always written inside a curved stroke:

stock   style   stop   most   next   just   lost   past   state   stores   starting

Circle S can be added to the **ST loop**:

tests   boasts   suggests   coasts   posts   guests   lasts   rests   bursts

Note that downward **R** is used at the end of an outline when immediately followed by the sound of **ST**.

The **ST** loop cannot be used when a vowel occurs between **S** and **T**, or when a vowel at the end of a word follows the sound of **ST**:

beset   bestow   gusset   gusto   cassettes

Read the above outlines and write them several times. Then read the following sentences and write them several times from dictation.

Exercise 30

1 ... (17)

47

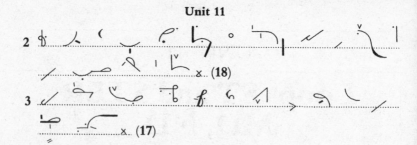

2

x. **(18)**

3

x. **(17)**

The sound **STER** is represented by a large loop, two-thirds the length of a normal length stroke, in the middle or at the end of an outline. **Circle S** can be added to the **STER loop**.

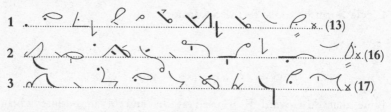

master   mastered   faster   posters   clusters   Leicester   roster

Read the above outlines and write them several times. Then read the following sentences and write them several times from dictation.

Exercise 31

1   x. **(13)**

2   x. **(16)**

3   x. **(17)**

Strokes **M** and **N** are halved and thickened to add the following sound of **D**:

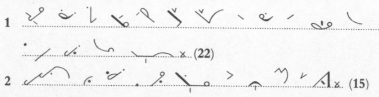

madam   made   mud   end   modernize   sends   standing   standard

Read the above outlines and write them several times. Then read the following sentences and write them several times from dictation.

Exercise 32

1

x. **(22)**

2   x. **(15)**

Unit 11

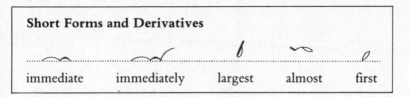

Short Forms and Derivatives

immediate   immediately   largest   almost   first

Phrases

at first first time for the first time first class as fast as just as

Note the omission of the word *the* in the phrase *for the first time*.

Exercise 33

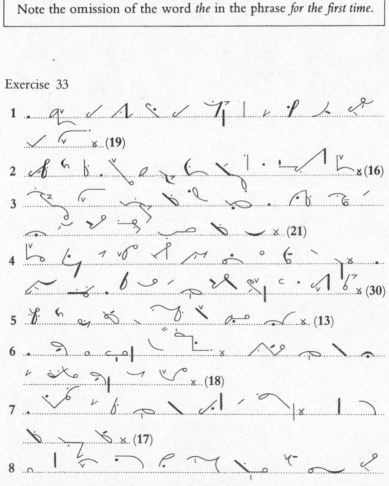

49

Unit 11

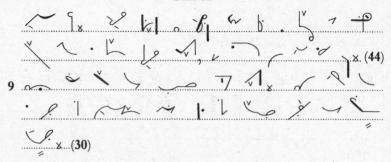

9

...x...(30)

Short Form and Phrase Drill

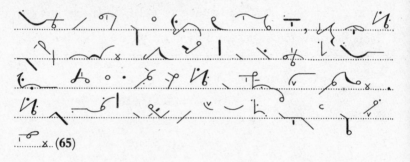

...x...(65)

R hook to straight strokes: PR, BR, TR, DR CHR, JR, KR, GR Circles and ST loop to hooks

A small hook at the beginning of a straight downstroke and the horizontals **K** and **G**, adds the sound of **R**. The hook is always written on the left-hand side of straight downstrokes, and underneath straight horizontals.

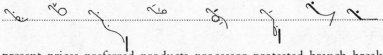

PR   BR   TR   DR   CHR   JR   KR   GR

The **hook R** is used *consonantally*, that is, the two consonants follow each other with no vowel between them. Write the hook first then the stroke:

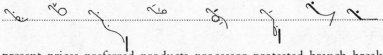

present prices preferred products processor protested branch break

trial   trouble   transfer   crossed   address   growth   aggravate

The **hook R** is used in the middle of an outline:

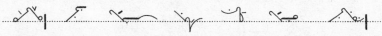

surprised regret programme petrol entrust progress represented

Read the above outlines and write them several times. Then read the following sentences and write them several times from dictation.

Exercise 34

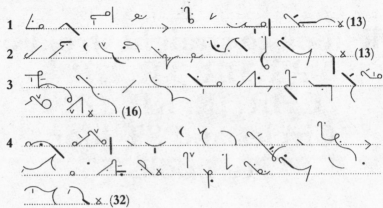

1   x (13)

2   x (13)

3   (16)

4   x (32)

The **hook R** is used *syllabically*:

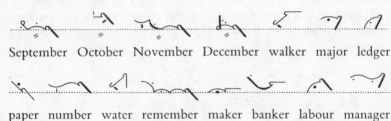

September October November December walker major ledger

paper number water remember maker banker labour manager

Read the above outlines and write them several times. Then read the following sentences and write them several times from dictation.

Exercise 35

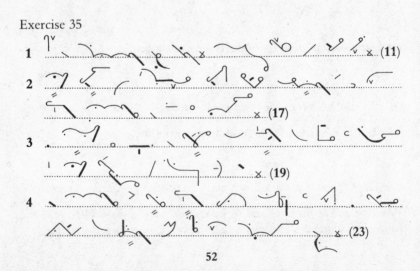

1   x (11)

2   x (17)

3   x (19)

4   x (23)

For words beginning with the sound **SPR-**, **STR-** or **SKR-** write a complete circle in the same direction as **hook R**: ⟍, ⟍ and ⟍:

spray   stress   straight   strike   strength   strong   scrape

When the sound **SKR** or **SGR** follows **D**, **P** or **B** the hook and circle are written:

describe   prescribe   subscribe

Read the above outlines and write them several times. Then read the following sentences and write them several times from dictation.

Exercise 36

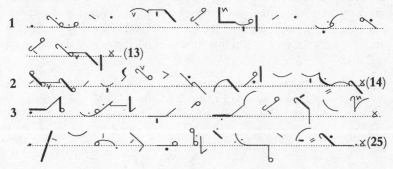

1 ....

.... x...**(13)**

2 .... x**(14)**

3 ....

.... x**(25)**

When a word begins with either **S**–vowel or **ST**–vowel followed by a straight stroke hooked for **R**, the **circle S** or **ST loop** is written on the same side of the stroke as the **hook R**.

supper   cider   sober   soccer   stutter   stoker   stagger   stopper

When **circle S** precedes **hook R** in the middle of an outline, the circle is written in the same direction as the **hook R**, with both the hook and the circle shown:

express   extra   destroy   demonstrate

Read the above outlines and write them several times. Then read the following sentences and write them several times from dictation.

Exercise 37

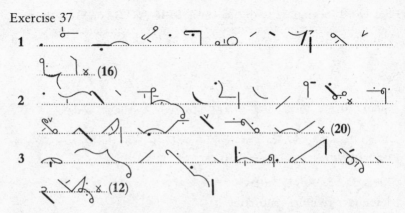

1 ... (16)

2 ... x (20)

3 ... x (12)

The L and R Hooks and stressed and unstressed syllables

In the English language all words of more than one syllable have stressed and unstressed syllables which means that a stressed syllable has more emphasis placed on it by pronouncing it louder than other syllables in the word. When pronouncing the word *perform*, for example, more emphasis is placed on the second syllable -*form* than on the first syllable *per-*. Therefore, the second syllable is the **stressed syllable**.

When the unstressed syllable **consonant–vowel–L** or **consonant–vowel–R** occurs in a word of more than one syllable, the **hook L** or the **hook R**, whichever is applicable, is used in the shorthand outline and the vowel occurring in this syllable is omitted. When the hook is used in a root outline, the hook is retained in **all** derivatives:

Hook L

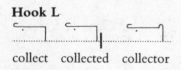

collect   collected   collector

Hook R

perform   performance   correct   corrected   portray

When the stressed syllable **consonant–vowel–L** or **consonant–vowel–R** occurs in a word of more than one syllable, the **hook L** or **hook R** is *not* used in the root outline or in derivatives:

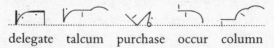

delegate   talcum   purchase   occur   column

The **hook L** or the **hook R** is *not* used for one syllable words containing **consonant–vowel–L–consonant** or **consonant–vowel–R–consonant**:

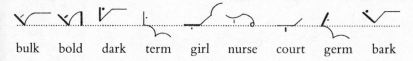

bulk   bold   dark   term   girl   nurse   court   germ   bark

---

Short Forms and Derivatives

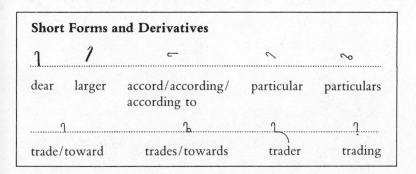

| dear | larger | accord/according/ according to | particular | particulars |

| trade/toward | trades/towards | trader | trading |

Phrases

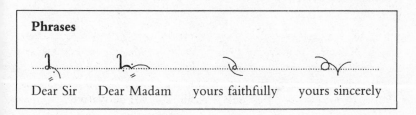

Dear Sir   Dear Madam   yours faithfully   yours sincerely

Intersections

When convenient intersect stroke **K** for *company* and strokes **K** and **L** joined for *company limited*:

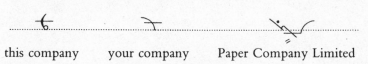

this company   your company   Paper Company Limited

Read the above short forms, phrases and intersections and write them several times. Then read the following sentences and write them several times from dictation.

Exercise 38

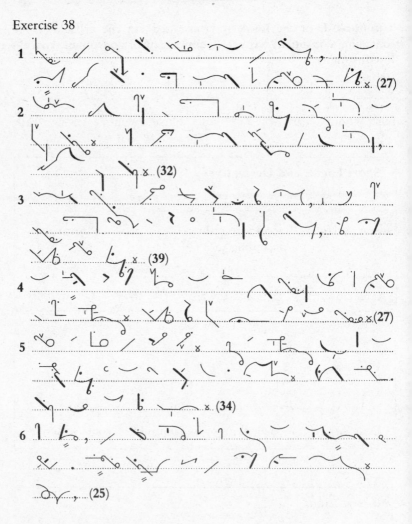

Short Form and Phrase Drill

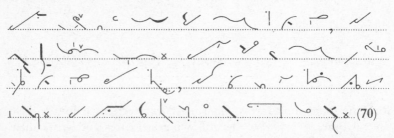

Third-place vowels Ē, Ĭ, ŌO, ŎO Position writing Stroke S (2) Stroke Z Diphones

In the following examples the first downstroke or upstroke is written *through* the line. These are known as *third-position* outlines.

The long sound of Ē (as in *please*) is represented by a heavy dot written in the third place at the *end* of a stroke, either before it or after it, wherever it is sounded:

please	pleases	deed	fee	feet/feat	treat	least	pieces	eats	these

she	see	seeing	ear	steal/steel	street	tree	each	lease

Read the above outlines and then write them several times.

When a third-place vowel occurs between two strokes it is written in the third place *before* the second stroke:

teachers	feel	read	cheapest	deeper	dealing	reached	fear	keep

people	clear	keyboard	legal	ream	weak/week	leaves	meal	team

Unit 13

Remember that in third-position outlines for words such as........ *meal* and .... *keep*, it is the first upstroke or downstroke that is written *through* the line.

Read the outlines on page 57 and write them several times. Then read the following sentences and write them several times from dictation.

Exercise 39

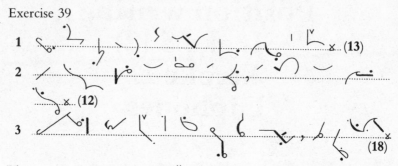

The sound of the short vowel Ĭ (as in *if*) is represented by a light dot written in third position. When a third-place vowel occurs between two strokes it is written in the third position *before* the second stroke:

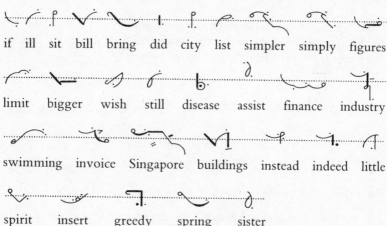

if ill sit bill bring did city list simpler simply figures

limit bigger wish still disease assist finance industry

swimming invoice Singapore buildings instead indeed little

spirit insert greedy spring sister

Read the above outlines and then write them several times.

When **hook L** or **hook R** is used in a root outline, the hook is retained in derivatives even though the stressed syllable may change:

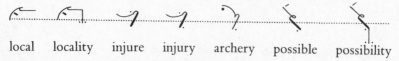

local locality injure injury archery possible possibility

58

Unit 13

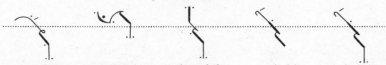

impossibility   availability   adaptability   probable   probability

Read the above outlines and write them several times. Then read the following sentences and write them several times from dictation.

Exercise 40

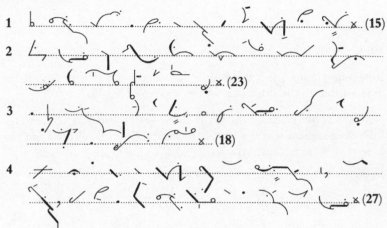

The long sound of $\overline{OO}$ (as in *blue*) is represented by a heavy dash written in third place:

blue truth July use lose/loose move group cool shoe food unit

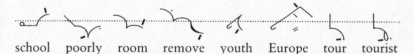

school   poorly   room   remove   youth   Europe   tour   tourist

Read the above outlines and write them several times. Then read the following sentences and write them several times from dictation.

Exercise 41

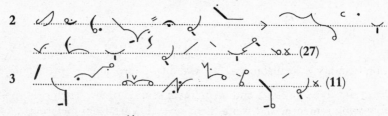

2 ... (27)

3 ... (11)

The short sound of **ŎO** (as in *book*) is represented by a light dash written in third place:

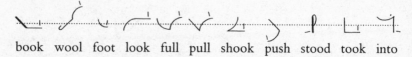

book wool foot look full pull shook push stood took into

Remember that when a third–place vowel occurs between two strokes it is written in the third place *before* the *second* stroke.

Read the above outlines and write them several times. Then read the following sentences and write them several times from dictation.

Exercise 42

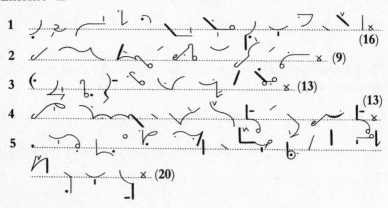

1 ... (16)

2 ... (9)

3 ... (13)

4 ... (13)

5 ... (20)

Position Writing

When the third-place vowel sound **Ē, Ĭ, ŌO** or **ŎO** is the first in a word, the first downstroke or upstroke is written through the line. When there is no downstroke or upstroke and the outline contains only horizontal strokes, the outline is written on the line:

increase good me miss cook include scheme need

Remember that it is the *first sounded vowel* in a word which determines the position of an outline:

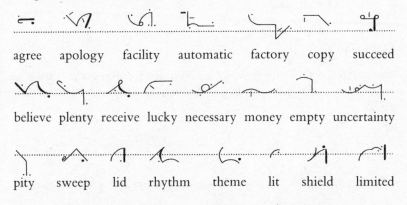

agree   apology   facility   automatic   factory   copy   succeed

believe plenty receive lucky necessary money empty uncertainty

pity   sweep   lid   rhythm   theme   lit   shield   limited

When a third-place vowel is sounded between a consonant and a **T** or **D** and the stroke has been halved to indicate the **T** or **D**, the vowel is written in third place immediately after the half-length stroke:

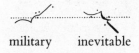

military   inevitable

When a third-place vowel occurs following a stroke followed by **circle S** or **ST loop and another stroke,** the vowel is written in third place *following* the stroke and *before* the **circle S** or **ST** loop:

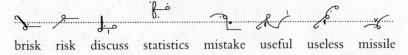

brisk risk discuss statistics mistake useful useless missile

Read the above outlines and write them several times. Then read the following sentences and write them several times from dictation.

Exercise 43

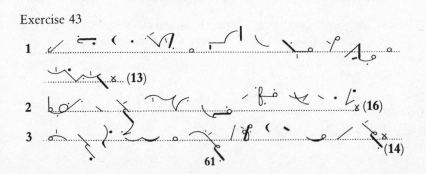

1 ... x (13)

2 ... x (16)

3 ... (14)

4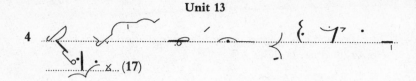

.... (17)

Stroke S

When **stroke S** is the first stroke in a root outline, the stroke is retained in compound words and derivatives formed by means of a prefix:

saw sawdust ice icebox escapable inescapable sea seasickness

Z is a thick curved downstroke ...... When **Z** is the first or only consonant sound in a word use **stroke Z**:

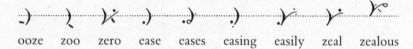

ooze zoo zero ease eases easing easily zeal zealous

When a vowel sound follows **S** or **Z** at the end of a word, **stroke S** or **Z** is used:

busy cosy lazy daisy posy rosy policy galaxy jealousy

Remember to write **circle S** for the sound of **S** or **Z** in the middle of an outline:

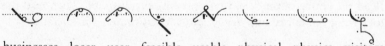

businesses loser user feasible usable physical physics visitors

Read the above outlines and write them several times. Then read the following sentences and write them several times from dictation.

Exercise 44

1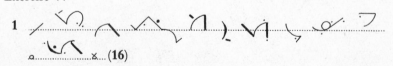

.... (16)

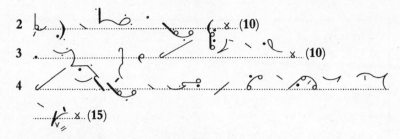

Double-Vowel Signs (Diphones)

When two vowel sounds follow each other, they are shown by the sign ν , making what is called a **diphone**. Write this sign in the position of the first vowel sound in the **diphone**:

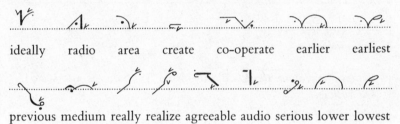

ideally   radio   area   create   co-operate   earlier   earliest

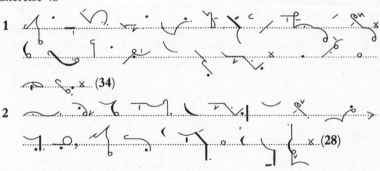

previous medium really realize agreeable audio serious lower lowest

Exercise 45

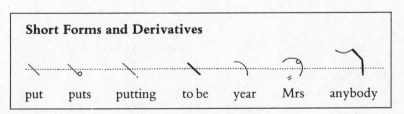

Short Forms and Derivatives

put   puts   putting   to be   year   Mrs   anybody

Phrases

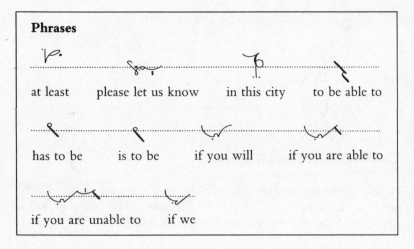

| at least | please let us know | in this city | to be able to |

| has to be | is to be | if you will | if you are able to |

| if you are unable to | if we |

Intersections

When convenient **stroke B** and **circle S** ⟍ is intersected for *business*:

| your business | our business | this business | good business |

Write the short forms, derivatives, phrases and intersections several times. Then read the following sentences several times, increasing your speed of *reading* each time before you write the sentences several times from dictation.

Exercise 46

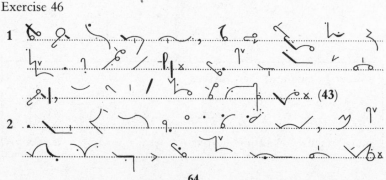

(43)

Unit 13

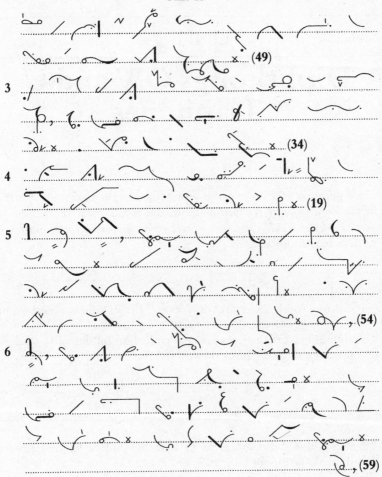

Short Form and Phrase Drill

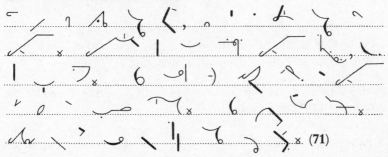

Diphthongs OW and U
Triphones

The diphthong **OW** (as in *out*) is represented by the sign ....⋀.... written in the *third place* at the *beginning*, in the *middle* or at the *end* of an outline. When **OW** is the first vowel sound in a word, the outline is written in the *third position*:

out outside south loud crowd council allow mouth shout stout

The diphthong **OW** is joined at the end of an outline after straight downstrokes and after most downward curves:

plough   ploughed   bow/bough   endow   vow   vowed

When **S** follows the sound of **OW** at the end of an outline, the diphthong **OW** cannot be joined:

ploughs   vows   bows/boughs   blouse   allows

Note: The outline for *now* is formed by joining the second half of the sign for **OW** to the end of stroke **N**: ⌒ *now*, and the diphthong **OW** is joined to **L** at the beginning of an outline: ⌒ *owl*.

A single straight downstroke may be halved for either **T** or **D** if the diphthong **OW** can be joined:

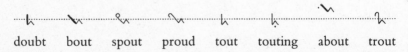

doubt   bout   spout   proud   tout   touting   about   trout

Unit 14

In one syllable words a *thin stroke* may be halved only for **T**, and a *thick stroke* may be halved only for **D** when the **OW** diphthong *cannot* be joined:

doubts   bouts   spouts   touts   shouts

A small tick added to the diphthong **OW** indicates any following vowel sound and the sign is called a **triphone**:

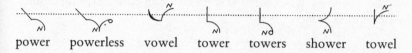

power   powerless   vowel   tower   towers   shower   towel

Read the outlines and write them several times. Then read the following sentences and write them several times from dictation.

Exercise 47

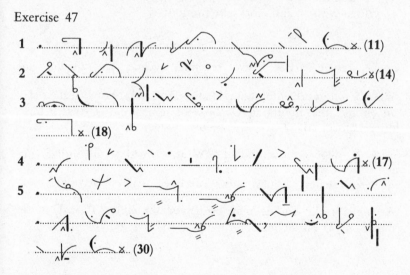

The diphthong **U** (as in *duty*) is represented by the sign ....ᴒ.... written in the *third place* in the *middle* or at the *end* of an outline. When **U** is the first vowel sound in a word, the outline is written in the *third position*:

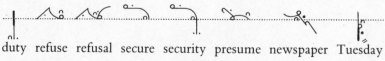

duty   refuse   refusal   secure   security   presume   newspaper   Tuesday

67

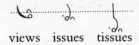

during accurate opportunity fortunate unfortunate assume volume

The diphthong **U** is joined at the *end* of an outline following strokes written downwards:

due few view viewed issue issued sue astute tissue

When **S** follows the sound of **U** at the *end* of an outline, the diphthong **U** cannot be joined:

views issues tissues

The **U** diphthong is joined *finally* following **K, G, M, N** and **L** and is written with an anti-clockwise motion:

queue rescue argue mew revenue avenue knew/new value

When **S** follows the diphthong **U** after **K, G, M, N** or **L** at the *end* of an outline, the diphthong **U** *cannot* be joined and is written in its original form:

queues rescues argues news avenues values accuse

A single stroke outline may be halved for either **T** or **D** if the diphthong **U** can be joined:

feud mute

In one syllable words a *thin stroke* may be halved only for **T** and a *thick stroke* may be halved only for **D** when the **U** diphthong *cannot* be joined:

feuds mutes

Unit 14

A small tick added to the diphthong **U** indicates any following vowel sound and the sign is called a **triphone**:

valuable fewer mutual duet duets individual situated graduate

When a diphthong or a diphone occurs in the syllable **consonant–diphthong/diphone–L**, or **consonant–diphthong/diphone–R**, the **hook L** or **hook R** is *not* used so that the diphthong or diphone may be written:

regulate regular circulate circular mixture fixture lecture lecturers

Read the above outlines and write them several times. Then read the following sentences and write them several times from dictation.

Exercise 48

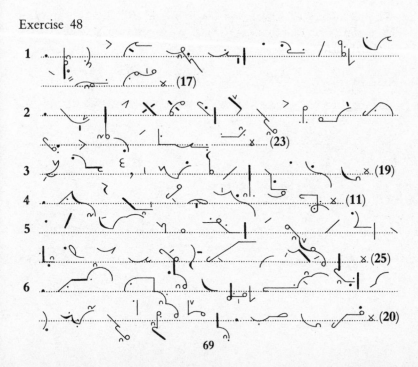

69

Short Forms and Derivatives

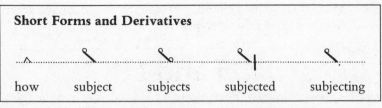

| how | subject | subjects | subjected | subjecting |

Phrases

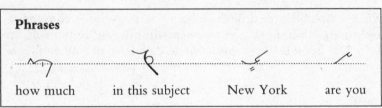

| how much | in this subject | New York | are you |

Read the above short forms and phrases and write them several times. Then read the following short form and phrase drill and write it several times from dictation.

Short Form and Phrase Drill

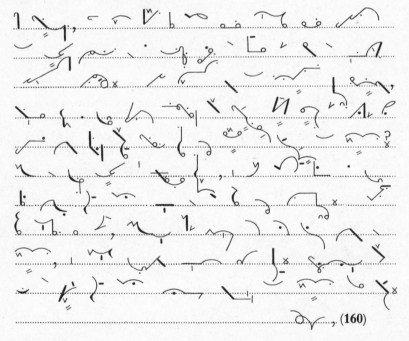

(160)

UNIT 15

ZH and H

The sound **ZH** (as in *usual*) is a thick curved downstroke 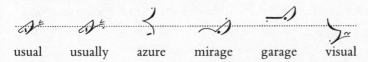:

usual   usually   azure   mirage   garage   visual

Read the above outlines and then write them several times. Then read the following sentences and write them several times from dictation.

Exercise 49

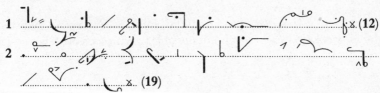

1 ... **(12)**

2 ...

... **(19)**

The sound of **H** is represented by the sign .... written *upwards*:

he   hope   happiness   high   higher   highlight   hotel   head   whose

heat   hurried   houses   habit   hero   herd   harsh   hard   harvest

perhaps   prohibit   adhere   hospital   harbour   hew/hue/Hugh

(*Note* the change of direction of the **U** diphthong.)

Read the above outlines and then write them several times.

71

Note the difference between the writing of **circle S** before upward **R**, and the writing of **H** as in: 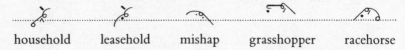 *sorry*, *high*.

When **S** occurs in the middle of a word immediately followed by **H**, the **H** is omitted from the outline:

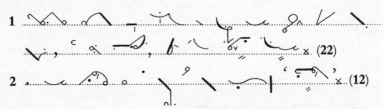

household   leasehold   mishap   grasshopper   racehorse

Read the above outlines and write them several times. Then read the following sentences and write them several times from dictation.

Exercise 50

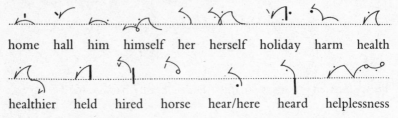

1 ... (22)

2 ... (12)

When **S** is the first consonant in a word, followed by a vowel followed by **H**, **stroke S** is used as it is not possible to write a **circle S** before **H**:

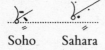

Soho   Sahara

A light tick written downwards from right to left 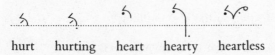 represents **H** when it is the first sound in a word and comes before **M**, **L** or downward **R**, or downward **R** circle **S**:

home   hall   him   himself   her   herself   holiday   harm   health

healthier   held   hired   horse   hear/here   heard   helplessness

In words of one syllable downward **R** following **tick H** may be halved for **T**. When downward **R** is used in a root outline, it is retained in derivatives:

hurt   hurting   heart   hearty   heartless

72

Exercise 51

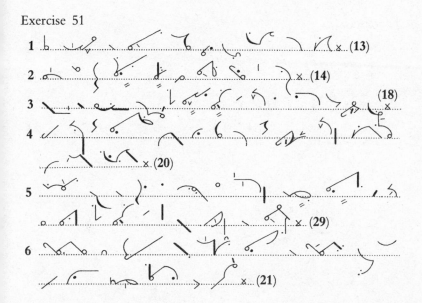

1 ... (13)

2 ... (14)

3 ... (18)

4 ...

... (20)

5 ...

... (29)

6 ...

... (21)

Remember to practise the phrases. Make sure you write them in their correct positions.

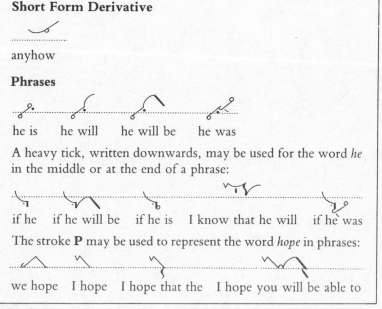

Short Form Derivative

anyhow

Phrases

he is   he will   he will be   he was

A heavy tick, written downwards, may be used for the word *he* in the middle or at the end of a phrase:

if he   if he will be   if he is   I know that he will   if he was

The stroke **P** may be used to represent the word *hope* in phrases:

we hope   I hope   I hope that the   I hope you will be able to

Read again the practice plan on page 4 *before* you begin work on Exercise 52.

Unit 15

Exercise 52

1 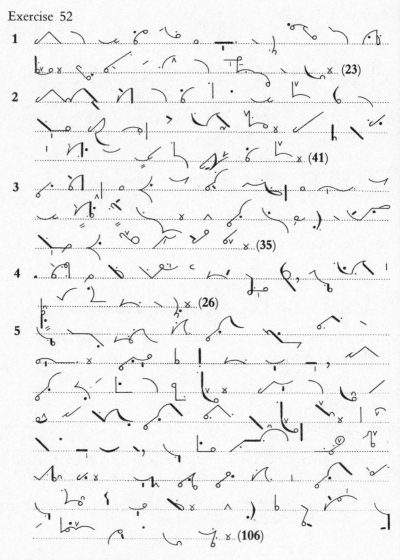 (23)

2 (41)

3 (35)

4 (26)

5 (106)

Short Form and Phrase Drill

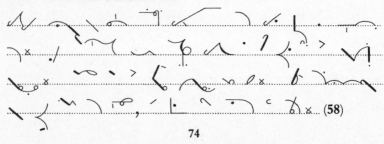 (58)

74

N hook to curved strokes

A *small* hook written inside the *end* of a curved stroke adds the final sound of **N**:

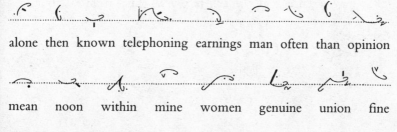

alone   then   known   telephoning   earnings   man   often   than   opinion

mean   noon   within   mine   women   genuine   union   fine

Circle S is written *inside* **hook N** at the end of a *curved* stroke for the final sound of **NZ**:

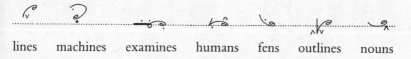

lines   machines   examines   humans   fens   outlines   nouns

Read the above outlines and write them several times. Then read the following sentences and write them several times from dictation.

Exercise 53

1 _____ x. (12)

2 _____

____ x. (15)

3 _____

____ x. (14)

After a curved stroke the sound of **NS** is represented by **stroke N** and **circle S** and the sound of **NSES** is represented by **stroke N** and **SES circle**:

fence   fences   announce   announces   balance   balances   allowance

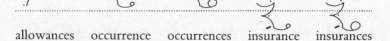

allowances   occurrence   occurrences   insurance   insurances

Read the above outlines and write them several times. Then read the following sentences and write them several times from dictation.

Exercise 54

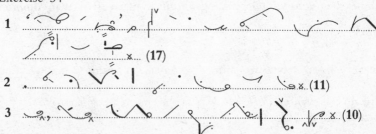

1 .... (17)

2 .... (11)

3 .... (10)

When a root outline is written with a curve followed by **hook N** and **circle S**, **stroke N** and **ZEZ circle** are used to represent a possessive case or plural:

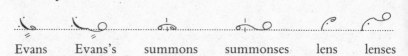

Evans   Evans's   summons   summonses   lens   lenses

A finally hooked thin or thick curved stroke is halved to add the following sound of **T** or **D**. The **circle S** is written inside the **hook N** at the end of half-length curved strokes for the *final* sound of **S** or **Z**:

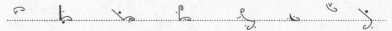

mind   demand   payments   settlement   sufficient   event   find   patient

Stroke N is always used at the end of an outline when **N** is followed by a sounded vowel:

funny   many   avenue   shiny   revenue

Unit 16

When a vowel occurs between the sound of **N** and **S** or the sound of **N** and **Z** at the end of a word, **stroke N** and **circle S/Z** are used:

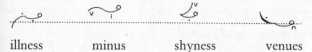

illness   minus   shyness   venues

In compound words, the root outlines for which are written with **hook N**, the hook is retained and the following part of the outline may be joined or disjoined—whichever is easier:

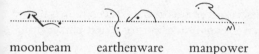

moonbeam   earthenware   manpower

Read the above outlines and write them several times. Then read the following sentences and write them several times from dictation.

Exercise 55

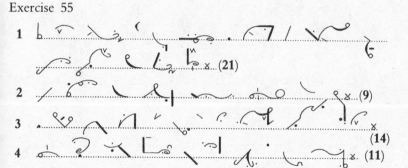

Phrases

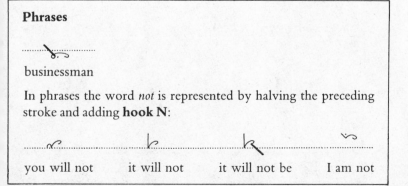

businessman

In phrases the word *not* is represented by halving the preceding stroke and adding **hook N**:

you will not   it will not   it will not be   I am not

77

Intersections

When convenient intersect downward **R** for *arrange, arranged, arrangement* and downward **R dot ING** for *arranging*:

this arrangement we will arrange I have arranged I am arranging

---

Read the phrases and intersections and write them several times before you read and write Exercise 56 and the short form and phrase drill.

Exercise 56

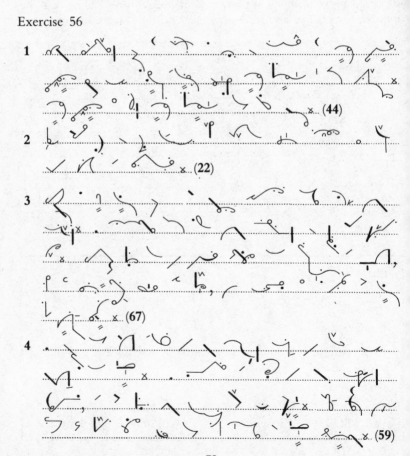

5
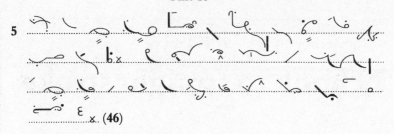

.... x. (46)

Short Form and Phrase Drill

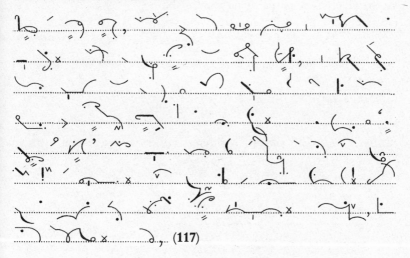

(117)

N hook to straight strokes

A *small* hook written at the *end* of a straight stroke on the opposite side to the **circle S** adds the final sound of **N**:

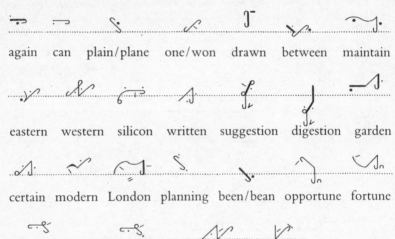

again   can   plain/plane   one/won   drawn   between   maintain

eastern   western   silicon   written   suggestion   digestion   garden

certain   modern   London   planning   been/bean   opportune   fortune

correspond   corresponding   return   turnings

Read the above outlines and write them several times. Then read the following sentences and write them several times from dictation.

Exercise 57

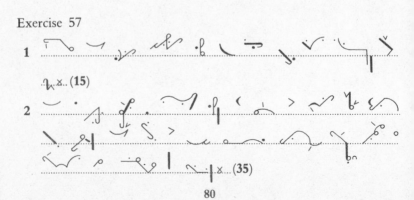

1   ....

.....x. **(15)**

2   ....

....

....x. **(35)**

Unit 17

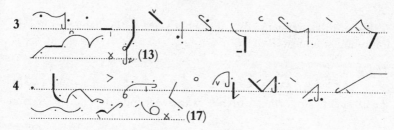

3 .... (13)

4 .... (17)

A *small* final circle written on the **hook N** *side* of a *straight* stroke represents the sound of **NS** or **NZ**:

begins   engines   turns   once   returns   bounce   trains   dance   saddens

diligence   joins   evidence   declines   assistance   attendance   expense

The final sound of **NSES, NZES, NSTER** or **NST** is added to a *straight* stroke by writing the *circle* or *loop* on the *same* side as the **hook N**:

bronzes   tenses   expenses   princesses   princes   spinster   against

Read the above outlines and write them several times. Then read the following sentences and write them several times from dictation.

Exercise 58

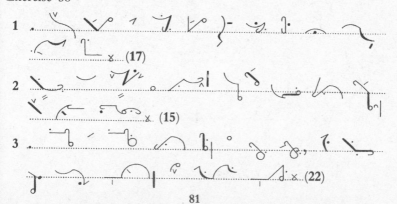

1 .... (17)

2 .... (15)

3 .... (22)

81

Unit 17

A thin or thick *straight* stroke *finally* hooked for **N** is halved to add the following sound of **T** or **D**:

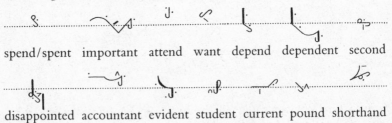

spend/spent   important   attend   want   depend   dependent   second

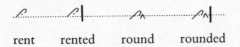

disappointed   accountant   evident   student   current   pound   shorthand

Upward **R** finally hooked for **N** is halved for the following sound of **T** or **D**:

rent   rented   round   rounded

The **circle S** is written on the **hook N** side of half-length straight strokes for the final sound of **NTS** or **NDZ**:

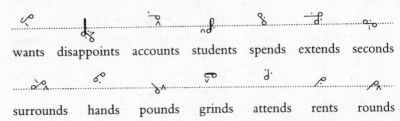

wants   disappoints   accounts   students   spends   extends   seconds

surrounds   hands   pounds   grinds   attends   rents   rounds

Read the above outlines and write them several times. Then read the following sentences and write them several times from dictation.

Exercise 59

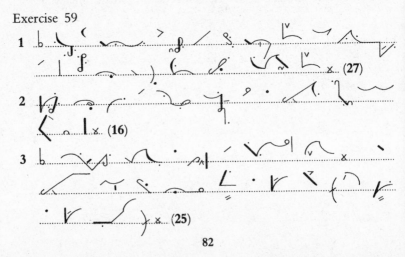

1 ... x. (27)

2 ... x. (16)

3 ... x. (25)

82

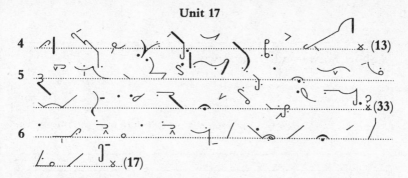

4 ... **x. (13)**

5 ... **x.(33)**

6 ... **x..(17)**

Stroke N is always used at the end of an outline when followed by a sounded vowel:

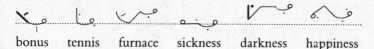

bony   tinny   rainy   deny   destiny   uncanny   canoe

When a vowel occurs between the sound of **N** and **S** or the sound of **N** and **Z** at the end of an outline, **stroke N** and **circle S/Z** are *always* used:

bonus   tennis   furnace   sickness   darkness   happiness

In *compound words*, the root outlines for which are written with **hook N**, the hook is retained and the following part of the outline may be joined or disjoined—whichever is easier:

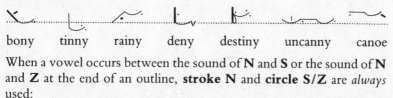

brainstorm   beanfeast   handwritten   handwriting   landlord

Read the above outlines and copy them several times. Then read the following paragraph and write it from dictation several times.

Exercise 60

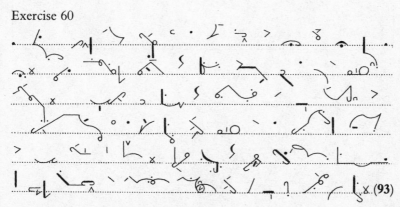

x.(93)

Short Forms and Derivatives

cannot	responsible/ responsibility	anyone	gentleman	gentlemen

Phrases

In a phrase the word *not* may be represented by halving the preceding stroke and adding **hook N**:

you are not   had not   do not   did not   they are not   I cannot

we cannot   I want   I went   it is certain   at once

In a phrase the words *been*, *than* and *own* are represented by adding **hook N**:

have been   had been   better than   our own   your own

When the phrase *are not* cannot be joined to a preceding stroke, the full outline must be used:

are not   we are not

Short Form and Phrase Drill

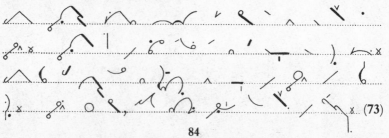

(73)

UNIT 18

Suffix -ment
Downward L
Suffix -ly

Suffix -MENT

When it is inconvenient to write the *suffix -MENT* ⌢., which it is after upstrokes and after **stroke N**, this suffix is represented by half-length **stroke N** ⌣... A third-place vowel occurring before the half-length **N** is written in the third position immediately after the stroke written before ⌣ representing **-MENT**:

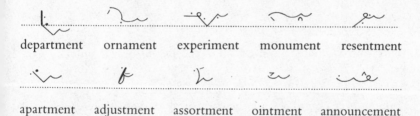

department   ornament   experiment   monument   resentment

apartment   adjustment   assortment   ointment   announcement

When the suffix **-MENT** is added to a root word, the outline for which is finally hooked for **N**, the hook is retained in derivatives containing the suffix **-MENT** and this suffix is represented by ⌣ or ⌢., whichever is convenient:

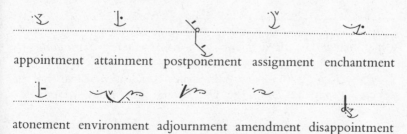

appointment   attainment   postponement   assignment   enchantment

atonement   environment   adjournment   amendment   disappointment

Read the above outlines and write them several times. Then read the following sentences and write them several times from dictation.

Exercise 61

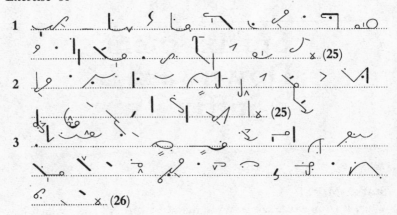

Downward L

L is *always* written downward after **stroke N, N halved** and **stroke NG**:

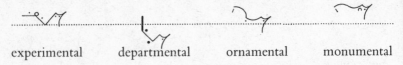

only unless annually unload until kneel nylon canal unlucky Nile

analysis unlicensed intellectual endless wrongly springlike strongly

When *half-length stroke N* is used for the syllable **-MENT** in a root outline, the *half-length* **stroke N** and **downward L** are used for **-MENTAL**:

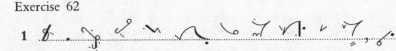

experimental   departmental   ornamental   monumental

Read the above outlines and write them several times. Then read the following sentences and write them several times from dictation.

Exercise 62

1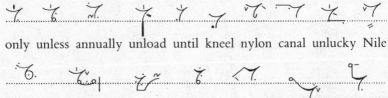

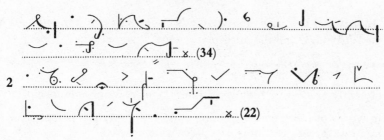

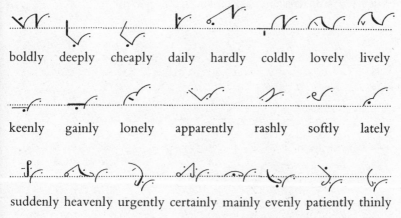

Suffix -LY

The suffix **-LY** is represented by upward **L** and the third-place **Ĭ** vowel. Hook **N** is retained in the root outline when followed by **-LY**:

boldly	deeply	cheaply	daily	hardly	coldly	lovely	lively

keenly	gainly	lonely	apparently	rashly	softly	lately

suddenly	heavenly	urgently	certainly	mainly	evenly	patiently	thinly

Read the above outlines and write them several times.

When a root outline ends with either **upward L** or **downward L**, or when a root outline is written with a final stroke hooked for **L,** the suffix **-LY** is formed by inserting the third-place **Ĭ** vowel:

actually	eventually	solely	wholly	singly	physically	locally

legally	totally	monumentally	experimentally	clinically

Read the above outlines and write them several times.

Downward L is used after **stroke N**, **N halved** and **stroke NG** for the suffix **-LY** and the third-place vowel **Ĭ** is inserted:

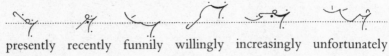

presently   recently   funnily   willingly   increasingly   unfortunately

In words of more than one syllable the suffix **-ALLY** is represented by **hook L** and the third-place **Ĭ** vowel is inserted:

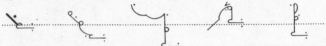

basically   specifically   fantastically   realistically   statistically

Read the above outlines and write them several times. Then read the following sentences and write them from dictation.

Exercise 63

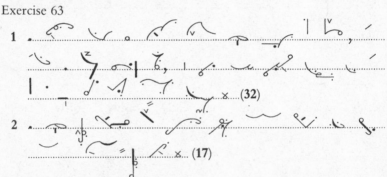

1. ... (32)

2. ... (17)

Short Form Derivatives

particularly   accordingly

Intersections

When convenient intersect **stroke D** for *department*:

your department   sales department   accounts department

Read and write the above short form derivatives and intersections. Then read Exercise 64, following the practice plan on page 4 so that you learn the outlines and increase your reading and writing speeds.

Exercise 64

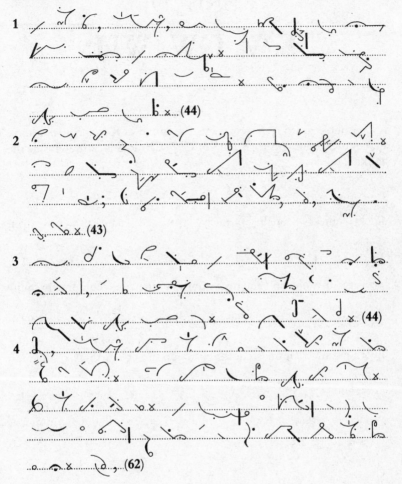

1

2 (43)

3 (44)

4 (62)

KW, GW, WH

A *large* hook added to **K** represents the sound of **KW** and a *large* hook added to **G** represents the sound of **GW**. **Circle S** is written inside the hook:

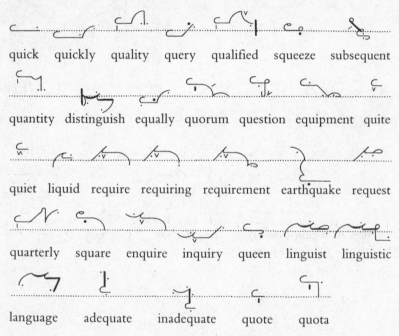

quick　quickly　quality　query　qualified　squeeze　subsequent

quantity　distinguish　equally　quorum　question　equipment　quite

quiet　liquid　require　requiring　requirement　earthquake　request

quarterly　square　enquire　inquiry　queen　linguist　linguistic

language　adequate　inadequate　quote　quota

Read the above outlines and then write them several times. Then read the following sentences and write them from dictation.

Exercise 65

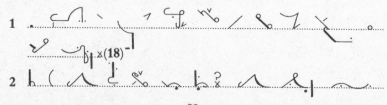

1

2

Unit 19

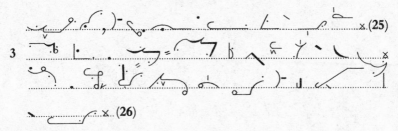

x.(25)

3

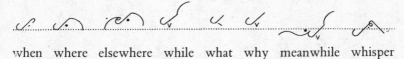

x.

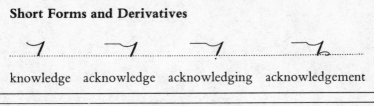

x.(26)

WH is a thin straight upstroke beginning with a large hook ⌒:

when   where   elsewhere   while   what   why   meanwhile   whisper

Read the above outlines and then write them several times.

Short Forms and Derivatives

knowledge   acknowledge   acknowledging   acknowledgement

Intersections

When convenient **stroke N** may be intersected for *enquire/ inquire, enquired/inquired, enquiry/inquiry*; and **upward R** may be intersected for *require, required, requirement*:

we will enquire/inquire   we have enquired/inquired

several enquiries/inquiries   your enquiry/inquiry

we shall require   will be required   your requirements

Read and write the above short forms, derivatives and intersections several times before you read Exercise 66 and then write it from dictation.

Exercise 66

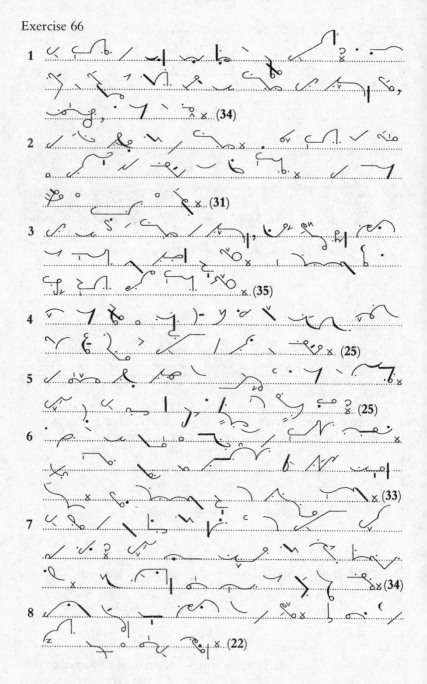

1 ... (34)

2 ... (31)

3 ... (35)

4 ... (25)

5 ... (25)

6 ... (33)

7 ... (34)

8 ... (22)

Short Form and Phrase Drill

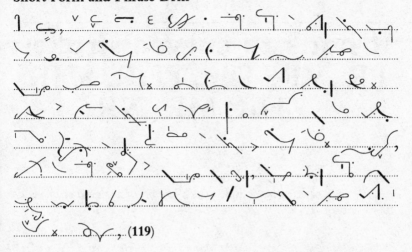

(119)

UNIT 20

R hook to curved strokes: FR, VR, Thr, THR, SHR, ZHR, MR, NR

A *small* hook written *inside* and at the *beginning* of a curved stroke adds the sound of **R**:

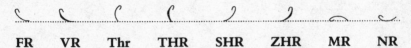

| FR | VR | Thr | THR | SHR | ZHR | MR | NR |

The **hook R** is used *consonantally*, that is, the two consonants follow each other with no vowel between them. Write the hook first, then the stroke:

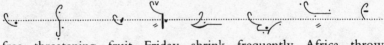

free   threatening   fruit   Friday   shrink   frequently   Africa   throw

Read the above outlines and write them several times. Then read the following sentences and write them several times from dictation.

Exercise 67

1   ... (17)

2   ... (12)

3   ... (19)

Unit 20

The **hook R** is used *syllabically* at the beginning, in the middle and at the end of an outline:

offer pressure energy measurement rumours different over otherwise

either favourable pleasure leisure manner/manor average mineral

When the unstressed syllable **consonant–vowel–R** occurs in a word, the **hook R** is used in the shorthand outline and the vowel occurring in this syllable is omitted:

forget   forgot   forgotten   advertise   foresee

When the **hook R** is used in a root outline, the hook is retained in all derivatives:

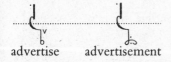

advertise   advertisement

Read the above outlines and write them several times. Then read the following sentences and write them several times from dictation.

Exercise 68

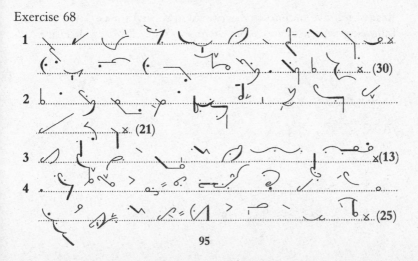

95

Circle S is written *inside* **hook R** attached to curved strokes. A finally sounded vowel may be added to the initially hooked curves:

savour savoury sever summery simmer suffer sooner deceiver

When a vowel occurs between a consonant and **R** in words of one syllable, the **hook R** is *not* used in the shorthand outline:

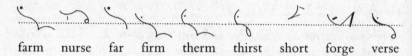

farm   nurse   far   firm   therm   thirst   short   forge   verse

When the *stressed* syllable **consonant–vowel–R** occurs in a word of more than one syllable, the **hook R** is *not* used in the shorthand outline:

Thursday fertile forecast murmur moral insure merchandise

When the **hook R** is *not* used in a root outline, the hook is *not* used in derivatives:

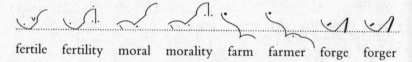

fertile fertility moral morality farm farmer forge forger

Read the above outlines and write them several times. Then read the following sentences and write them several times from dictation.

Exercise 69

1 .... x. **(22)**

2 .... x. **(18)**

The initially hooked curves **FR, VR, Thr, THR** are *always* reversed when immediately following upstrokes and horizontals. The reverse forms are written ⟍ ⟍ ⟩ ⟩ :

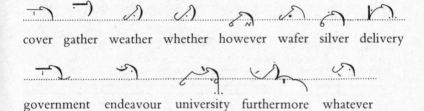

cover   gather   weather   whether   however   wafer   silver   delivery

government   endeavour   university   furthermore   whatever

When a diphthong or a diphone occurs in the *unstressed* syllable **consonant–diphthong/diphone–R**, the hook form is *not* used so that the diphthong or diphone may be written:

healthier   wealthier   junior

Read the above outlines and write them several times.

When the consonant **R** occurs in the spelling of a word, the **R** must be represented in the shorthand outline as a consonant, either in upward form or in downward form, or as a hook. The presence of **R** in a word has a modifying effect upon a preceding vowel. Please re-read page xiv of the *Introduction* before you begin work on Exercises 70 and 71.

Exercise 70

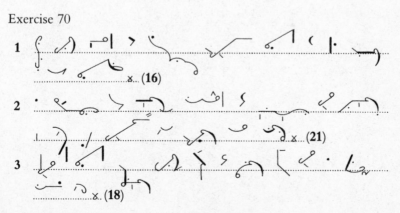

Short Forms and Derivatives

together	altogether	satisfactory	very	there/their	more

before	from	commercial/commercially

Phrases

very little	very much	there is	there are	there will be

there is no	there are no	I gather	more than	sooner than

Exercise 71

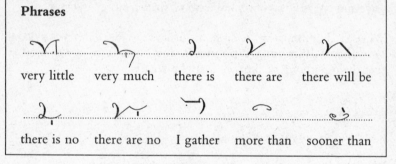

1 .... **(35)**

2 .... **(41)**

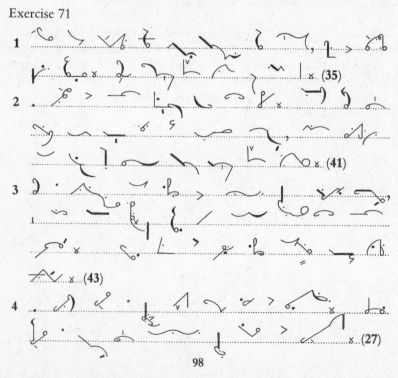

3 .... **(43)**

4 .... **(27)**

5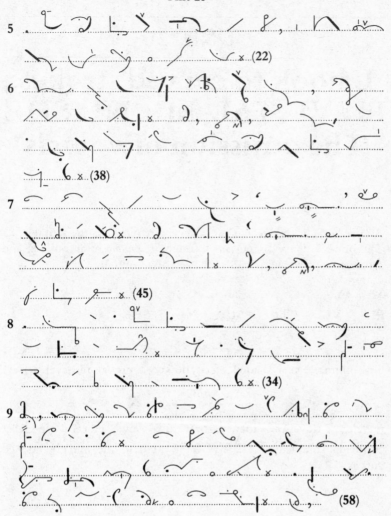

(22)

6 **(38)**

7 **(45)**

8 **(34)**

9 **(58)**

Short Form and Phrase Drill

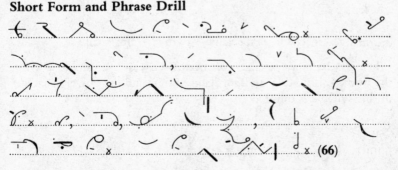

(66)

L hook to curved strokes: FL, VL, ThL, ML, NL, SHL
The omission of vowels

A *large* hook at the *beginning* of a curved stroke adds the sound of **L**. The **hook L** is used *consonantally* at the *beginning* of an outline, and *syllabically* in the *middle* and at the *end* of an outline:

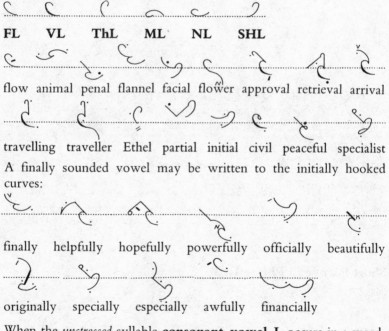

FL   VL   ThL   ML   NL   SHL

flow animal penal flannel facial flower approval retrieval arrival

travelling traveller Ethel partial initial civil peaceful specialist

A finally sounded vowel may be written to the initially hooked curves:

finally helpfully hopefully powerfully officially beautifully

originally specially especially awfully financially

When the *unstressed* syllable **consonant–vowel–L** occurs in a word, the **hook L** is used in the shorthand outline and the vowel occurring in this syllable is omitted:

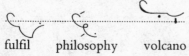

fulfil   philosophy   volcano

When the **hook L** is used in a *root outline*, the hook is retained in derivatives:

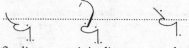

finality   originality   penalty

When a vowel occurs between a consonant and **L** in words of one syllable, the **hook L** is *not* used in the shorthand outline:

film   full   milk   vale

When the *stressed* syllable **consonant–vowel–L** occurs in a word of more than one syllable, the **hook L** is *not* used in the shorthand outline:

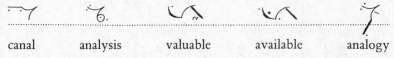

canal   analysis   valuable   available   analogy

When the **hook L** is not used in a root outline, the hook is not used in derivatives.

When a diphthong, triphone or a diphone occurs in the unstressed syllable, **consonant–diphthong/triphone/diphone–L,** the hook form is *not* used so that the diphthong, triphone or diphone may be written:

genial   menial   manual

Read the above outlines and then write them several times. Then read the following sentences and write them several times from dictation.

Exercise 72

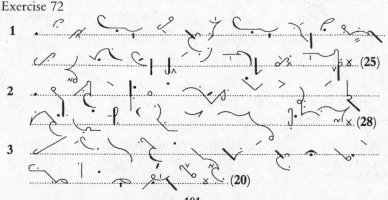

1 ... **(25)**

2 ... **(28)**

3 ... **(20)**

101

4 .... x. (11)

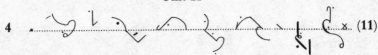

The initially hooked curves **FL** and **VL** are *always* reversed when immediately following upstrokes and horizontals. The reverse forms are written .... :

reflects marvellous level novel naval rival rivals removal

Read the above outlines and then write them several times.

Short Forms and Derivatives

enlarge   enlarged   enlarges   enlarging   enlarger   enlargement

influential   thankful

Phrases and Intersections

as early as possible   as soon as   as soon as it is

as soon as possible   as soon as we can   it is possible

it is not possible   United States   United States of America

Note that when convenient stroke **Th** for *month* may be intersected or joined, whichever is convenient:

some months   next month   six months   each month

Read and write the above short forms, phrases and intersections several times before you read Exercise 73 and then write it from dictation.

Exercise 73

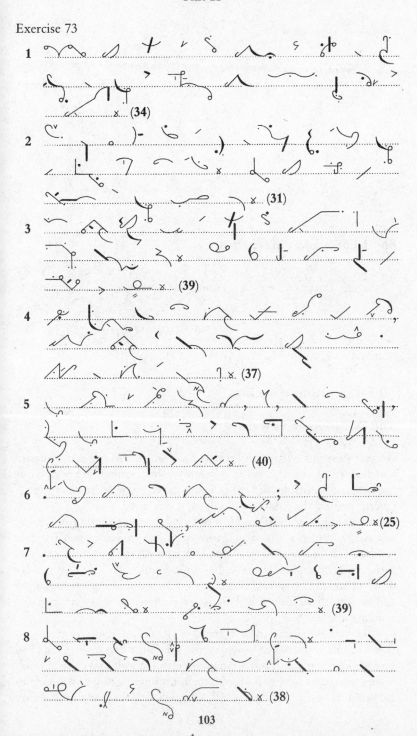

1 ... (34)

2 ... (31)

3 ... (39)

4 ... (37)

5 ... (40)

6 ... (25)

7 ... (39)

8 ... (38)

9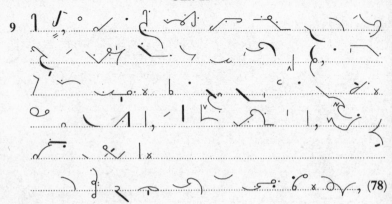

(78)

Short Form and Phrase Drill

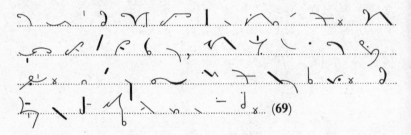

(69)

The Omission of Vowels

Correct position writing in Pitman 2000 Shorthand is a most important feature of the system. It is essential that outlines are written in their correct positions and the position in which to write an outline is determined by the first vowel sound in the word.

In your study of shorthand it is essential to know all the vowel signs and the correct place in which to write them in an outline. For this reason all the outlines in this book this far with the exception of short forms and some phrases, have the vowel signs included. You will by now appreciate, however, that many outlines can be easily recognized and read without any vowel signs, or perhaps with just an essential one being written.

When taking dictation at a speed well within your control, you should place most of the vowel signs. When the dictation is found to be fast, insert only a few essential vowels such as initial or final ones. With experience you will know which outlines need a vowel sign to aid rapid transcription. In general, you will find that long outlines are quite distinctive and do not need vowels at all. Short outlines, with perhaps only one consonant stroke, or a half-length stroke, must have a vowel sign. It is very important to place the diphthongs I, OI, OW, U and the triphones and diphones whenever they occur.

Always complete the consonant strokes for every outline. They are the skeleton of a word. When you have time, or know it to be necessary, add in the further detail—the vowel.

Essential vowel signs only will now be shown to assist you to read the shorthand quickly. If you have difficulty in reading an outline in your notes because there is no vowel sign, you must remember to insert one (or more) the next time you write that outline; but make sure you always write each outline in its correct position.

Now, read all this again. It is *the key to your success*.

F and V hook
Figures

A *small* hook written at the *end* of a *straight* stroke on the **circle S** side represents the sound of **F** or **V** when there is no finally sounded vowel. A finally hooked stroke may be halved for **T** or **D**:

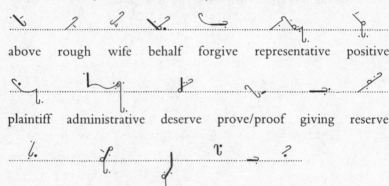

above   rough   wife   behalf   forgive   representative   positive

plaintiff   administrative   deserve   prove/proof   giving   reserve

achieving   suggestive   digestive   draft   gift   raft

Read and copy the above outlines several times. Then write the following sentences several times from dictation.

Exercise 74

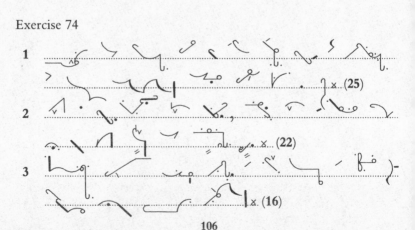

1 .... x. (25)

2 .... x. (22)

3 .... x. (16)

A final **S/Z circle** is written inside the **hook F** or **hook V**:

serves   deserves   proves   gives   reserves   relatives   halves   drifts

Read and copy the above outlines several times. Then write the following sentences several times from dictation.

Exercise 75

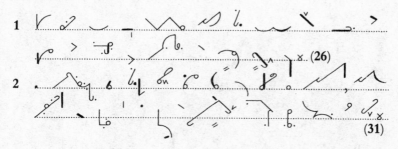

1

2

(26)

(31)

When the sound of **F** or **V** is followed by a finally sounded vowel or diphthong, the **stroke F** or **V** is *always* used:

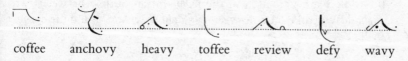

coffee   anchovy   heavy   toffee   review   defy   wavy

Read the above outlines several times then write the following sentences several times from dictation.

Exercise 76

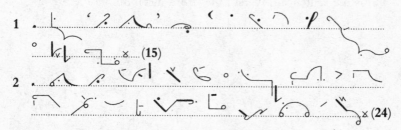

1

(15)

2

(24)

When a vowel, diphthong, triphone or diphone occurs between *final* **F** or **V** and **S, Z, SEZ** or **ZEZ** the **stroke F** or **V** and circle are used because a vowel, diphthong, triphone or diphone cannot be read between a final hook and a circle:

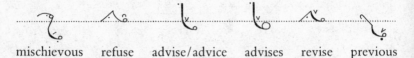

mischievous   refuse   advise/advice   advises   revise   previous

Read and copy the above outlines several times. Then write the following sentences several times from dictation.

Exercise 77

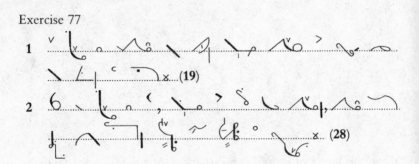

The **hook F** or **V** is used in the *middle* of an outline between two *straight* downstrokes and between a *straight* downstroke and the curves **Th, S, Z**:

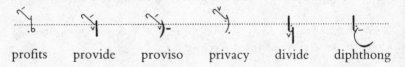

profits   provide   proviso   privacy   divide   diphthong

Read and copy the above outlines several times. Then write the following sentences several times from dictation.

Exercise 78

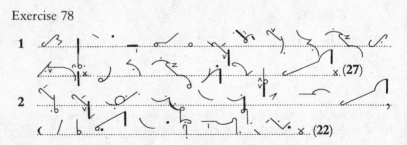

The **hook F** or **V** is used in the *middle* of an outline between a straight downstroke and the horizontals **K, G,** and **N**:

define   advancement   advantage   definitely   traffic   defect

Read and copy the above outlines several times. Then write the following sentences several times from dictation.

Exercise 79

1   **(21)**

2   **(21)**

The **hook F** or **V** is used in the *middle* of an outline between two *straight* horizontal strokes:

graphic   geographic   lithographic   photographic

Read the above outlines and write them several times. Then read the following sentences and write them several times from dictation.

Exercise 80

1   **(14)**

2   **(21)**

In derivative and compound words, the root outlines of which are written with the **hook V** *finally*, the hook is retained:

active   activity   captive   captivity   festive   festivity

When a root outline ends with **hook F** or **hook V**, the curves **F** and **V** initially hooked for either **R** or **L** are written for the *unstressed* syllables **er**, **al**, **iy**:

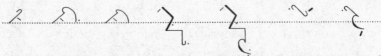

rough   roughly   rougher   objective   objectively   approve   approval

Read the above outlines and copy them. Then read the following paragraph and write it from dictation several times.

Exercise 81

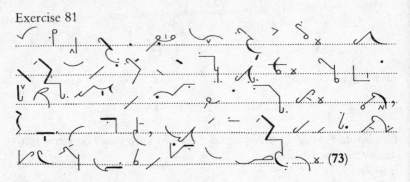

.x. (73)

Figures

With the exception of 0 and 8, the figures 1 to 10 and round numbers are best written as shorthand outlines in continuous matter:

1   2   3   4   5   6   7   9   10   20   30   40

All other numbers are represented by Arabic numerals.

Use stroke **N** for hundred: 500   **Th** for thousand: 3,000

Sums of money   £7,000   £740.10

M for million: 2,900,000 tons/tonnes.

Times of day: 1800 hours, 7 a.m., 5 p.m.

Read the following sentences and write them from dictation several times.

Exercise 82

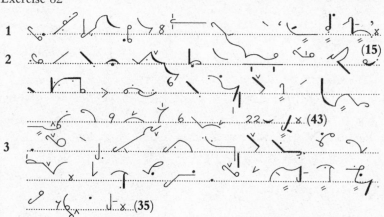

Short Forms and Derivatives

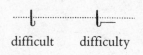

difficult   difficulty

Phrases

The **F** and **V** hook is used to represent the words *of*, *off*, or *have* in phrases:

type of lack of number of out of rate of sort of member of

better off set off you have who have not which have not

Tick the can be added to the **F** or **V** hook:

part of the   in spite of the   instead of the   advantage of the

---

Read and write the above short forms and phrases several times before you read Exercise 83 and then write it from dictation.

Exercise 83

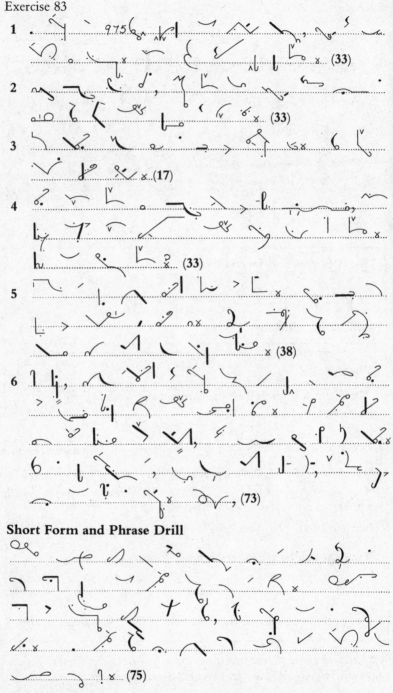

1 .... 975 .... (33)

2 .... (33)

3 .... (17)

4 .... (33)

5 .... (38)

6 .... (73)

Short Form and Phrase Drill

.... (75)

Double-length strokes

All curved strokes are *doubled* in length to represent the addition of the syllables **–TER**, **–DER**, **–THER** and **–TURE**. When the first consonant of an outline to be doubled commences with a downward curve, the outline begins in the same position as a stroke of ordinary length written to the line:

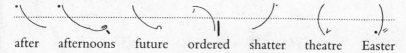

after   afternoons   future   ordered   shatter   theatre   Easter

When the doubling principle is applied to **upward L, M** and **N,** the position of the respective outline is determined by the first sounded vowel in the word:

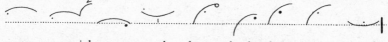

matter   material   metre   another   letters   leader   later   leather   entered

moderate alternative interrupt interview understanding natural neither

The doubling of curved strokes also applies to the *middle* and to the *end* of an outline, and the first sounded vowel in the word determines the position of the outline:

calculator   premature   signature   builder   furniture   bilateral

The double-length curves are used when they contain an initial hook or a final hook:

flatter   remainder   founder   vendor   inventor   islander   calendar

Doubling is *not* used when there is a finally sounded vowel:

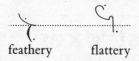

feathery   flattery

Read the outlines on page 113 and write them several times. Then read the following sentences and write them several times from dictation.

Exercise 84

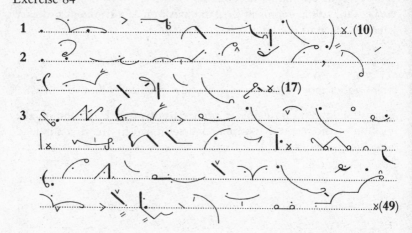

1 .... **(10)**

2 ....
.... **(17)**

3 ....
| **x** ....
....
....**(49)**

Straight strokes are *doubled* in length to represent the sounds of **-TER, -DER, -THER** and **-TURE** when they follow another stroke, or have a final hook:

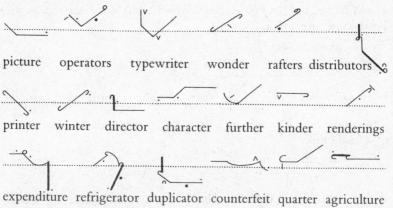

picture   operators   typewriter   wonder   rafters distributors

printer   winter   director   character   further   kinder   renderings

expenditure refrigerator duplicator counterfeit quarter agriculture

A straight stroke is *not* doubled if the doubling would produce two strokes of unequal length without an angle:

factor   navigator   victor

The doubling principle applied to straight strokes is *not* used in the middle of an outline as the doubling of a stroke would not be recognizable:

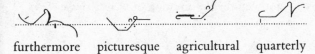

furthermore   picturesque   agricultural   quarterly

When the final syllable **-TURE** cannot be represented by doubling, the syllable is represented by **T** and **downward R**:

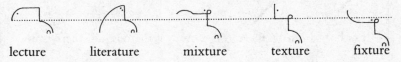

lecture   literature   mixture   texture   fixture

Read the above outlines and write them several times. Then read the following sentences and write them several times from dictation.

Exercise 85

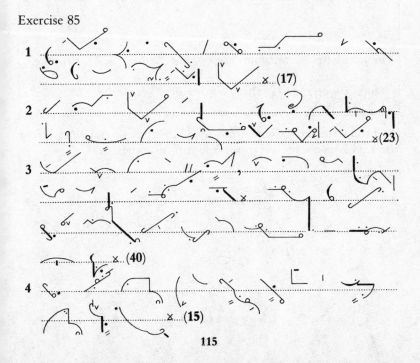

Short Forms

therefore wonderful/wonderfully January

Phrases

A stroke may be doubled for the addition of *there/their* or *other*:

I have been I have been there I know I know there is

I can be I can be there if there if there is if there is no

I think there is some other way in other ways your order

in your letter for your letter their letter later than the

Note: *for there/their* is always written

Read and write the above short forms and phrases several times before you read Exercise 86 and then write it from dictation.

Exercise 86

1

(42)

2

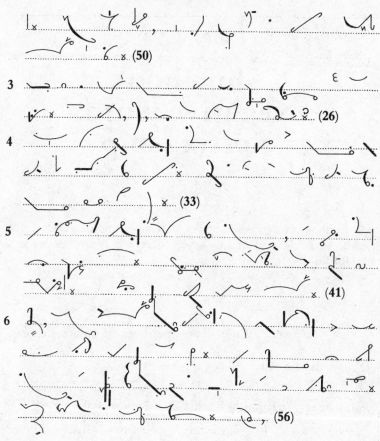

Short Form and Phrase Drill

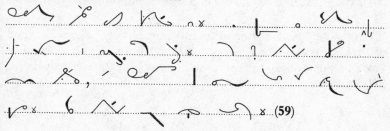

UNIT 24

Shun hook
Negative words
Suffix -ship

A *large* hook written *inside* curves adds the sound of **SHUN**, in the middle or at the end of an outline. **Circle S** is written inside the **SHUN hook**:

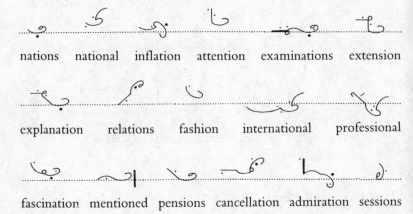

nations   national   inflation   attention   examinations   extension

explanation   relations   fashion   international   professional

fascination   mentioned   pensions   cancellation   admiration   sessions

When the *third-place* **dot** vowel occurs immediately before the sound of **SHUN**, it is written *inside* the **SHUN hook**. Other third-place vowels, diphthongs, triphones or diphones are written *outside* the **SHUN hook**.

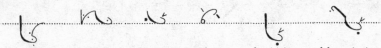

divisional   television   aviation   solution   deviation   abbreviation

Outlines for words ending in *-ble* are generally written with the hooked stroke ⟍, but *after* the **SHUN hook** it is necessary to write

118

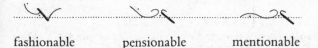...joined to the **SHUN hook**, or to disjoin written close to the **SHUN hook** as in:

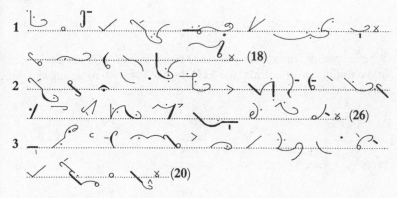

fashionable   pensionable   mentionable

Read the above outlines and write them several times. Then read the following sentences and write them several times from dictation.

Exercise 87

1 ... (18)

2 ... (26)

3 ... (20)

The **SHUN hook** is written at the *end* of a straight stroke on the side *opposite* to the vowel sounded immediately before **SHUN**. **Circle S** is written *inside* the **SHUN hook**:

operation variation co-operation moderation dedication occasions

education educational metrication medication application

When the **SHUN hook** is written to a *simple straight stroke* and there is no vowel occurring between the consonant and the sound of **SHUN**, the **SHUN** is written on the side of the straight stroke that will not imply the presence of a vowel immediately before **SHUN**:

attraction dictionary directions actions portion function distinction

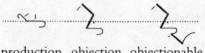

production   objection   objectionable

The **SHUN hook** is written on the right-hand side of simple **T, D** or **J** as a vowel always occurs between **T, D** or **J** and **SHUN**. Therefore, vowel indication is unnecessary:

additional   quotation   graduation   optician   magician   tradition

When a straight stroke has a circle or hook written at the beginning or in the middle of an outline, the **SHUN** hook is written on the *opposite* side to the circle or hook to balance the outline:

sections   station   exhibition   collection   corporation   celebrations

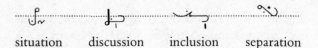

situation   discussion   inclusion   separation

Sometimes it is necessary to write the **SHUN hook** on the *same* side as the beginning circle or hook so that another stroke may be joined to **SHUN**:

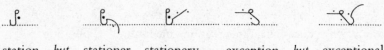

station   *but*   stationer   stationery   exception   *but*   exceptional

After ＼＿, ＼＿, ＼＿, ＼＿, ⌒ *or* ⌒ the **SHUN hook** is written away from the curve, to balance the outline:

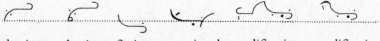

election   selection   fiction   vocational   qualification   modification

120

When the sound of **SHUN** occurs in the middle of a word and is followed by a vowel and **ST**, the **SHUN hook** is not used and **stroke SH, stroke N** and **ST loop** are written:

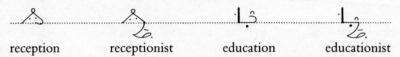

reception   receptionist   education   educationist

Read the above outlines and write them several times. Then read the following sentences and write them several times from dictation.

Exercise 88

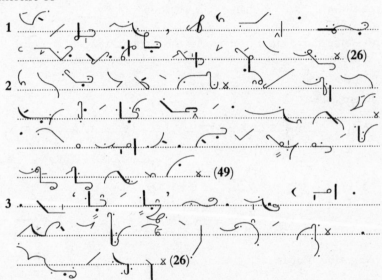

When the sound of **SHUN** follows the **S/Z circle** it is represented by a *small* hook written opposite the circle. This hook is written by continuing from the circle on the other side of the stroke. Third-position vowels occurring before **SHUN** are indicated. **Circle S** may be added to **S/Z–SHUN**:

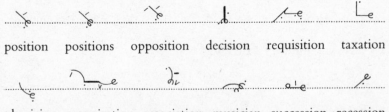

position   positions   opposition   decision   requisition   taxation

physician   organization   association   musician   succession   recession

When the sound of **S/Z–SHUN** is followed by **L,** a disjoined **upward L** is written close to the root outline:

positional   suppositional   processional   sensational   recessional

The sound **SHUN** following circle **NS/NZ** is shown by extending the circle to form a hook on the right-hand side of the stroke:

transition   transitional   dispensation

Read the above outlines and write them several times. Then read the following sentences and write them several times from dictation.

Exercise 89

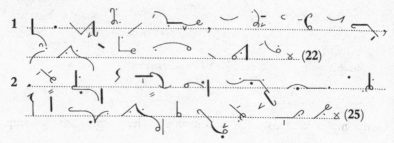

Negative Words

Words which have the prefix **IL-, IM-, IN-, IR-, UN-** are represented as follows:

By writing the **downward R** before the root outline:

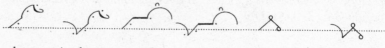

relevant   irrelevant   regular   irregular   responsible   irresponsible

By repeating the **L** or **M** or **N**:

legal   illegal   material   immaterial   known   unknown   necessary

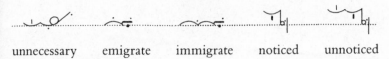

unnecessary   emigrate   immigrate   noticed   unnoticed

Other negative words are written:

patient impatient reliable unreliable fortunately unfortunately

When the prefix **IN-** means '*not*', **stroke N** is used:

different indifferent decision indecision dependent independent

Suffix -SHIP

The suffix **-SHIP** is represented by a joined or disjoined **stroke SH**. The **stroke SH** is usually joined to the preceding stroke, but when it is not possible to do so, or where the joining would result in an unreadable outline, the **stroke SH** is disjoined:

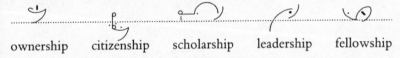

ownership   citizenship   scholarship   leadership   fellowship

The **hook N**, used finally in a root word, is retained in derivatives containing the suffix **-SHIP**:

friendship   chairmanship   penmanship

Read the above outlines and write them several times. Then read the following sentences and write them several times from dictation:

Exercise 90

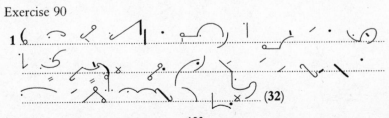

1

(32)

2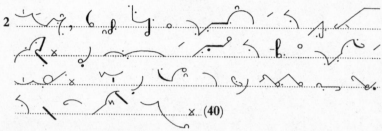

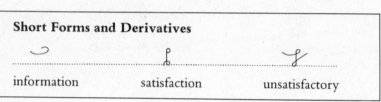

x (40)

Short Forms and Derivatives

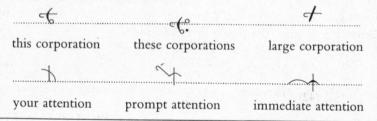

information   satisfaction   unsatisfactory

Intersections

When convenient **KR** may be intersected for *corporation*, and **T** may be intersected for *attention*:

this corporation   these corporations   large corporation

your attention   prompt attention   immediate attention

Read and write the above short forms, derivatives and intersections several times before you read Exercise 91 and then write it from dictation.

Exercise 91

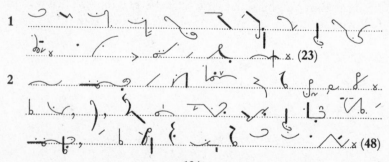

1 ....
.... x (23)

2 ....
....
.... x (48)

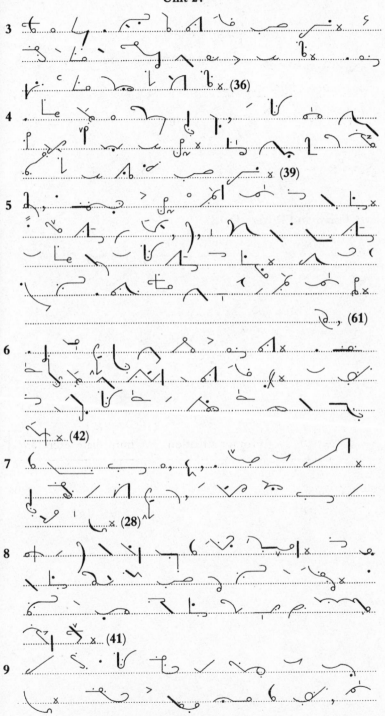

125

Unit 24

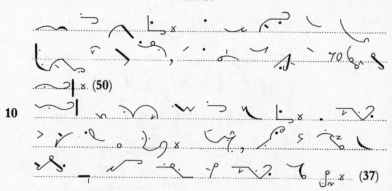

(50)

10

(37)

Short Form and Phrase Drill

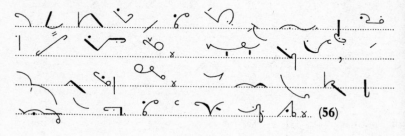

(56)

Dot CON, COM
Disjoining for CON,
COM, CUM, COG
Disjoined half-length T

The sounds **CON** and **COM** at the *beginning* of a word are represented by a dot written immediately before the beginning of the first stroke in the outline. The position of the outline is determined by the first vowel sound *following* **CON** or **COM**:

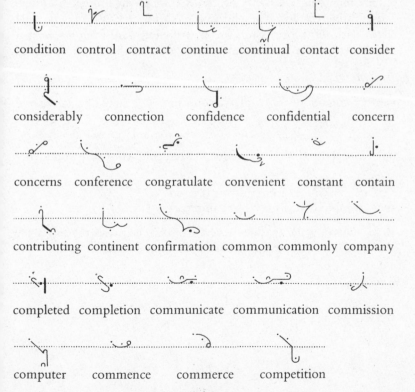

condition control contract continue continual contact consider

considerably connection confidence confidential concern

concerns conference congratulate convenient constant contain

contributing continent confirmation common commonly company

completed completion communicate communication commission

computer commence commerce competition

Unit 25

In the *middle* of a word the sound of **CON, COM, CUM** or **COG** is represented by writing the stroke immediately following any of these sounds close to the preceding stroke and omitting the dot:

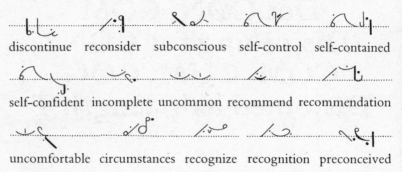

discontinue   reconsider   subconscious   self-control   self-contained

self-confident   incomplete   uncommon   recommend   recommendation

uncomfortable   circumstances   recognize   recognition   preconceived

incongruous   circumference

In phrases **CON** or **COM** may be indicated by writing the part of the outline following the **CON** or **COM** close to the preceding outline and omitting the dot. The omission of **CON** or **COM** may be used after a dash short form when this is written upwards, but *not* when a dash short form is written downwards *nor* after the dot short forms:

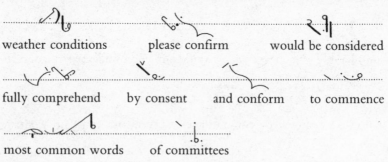

weather conditions   please confirm   would be considered

fully comprehend   by consent   and conform   to commence

most common words   of committees

Read and copy the outlines several times. Then read the following sentences and write them several times from dictation.

Exercise 92

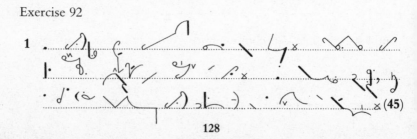

1

×(45)

128

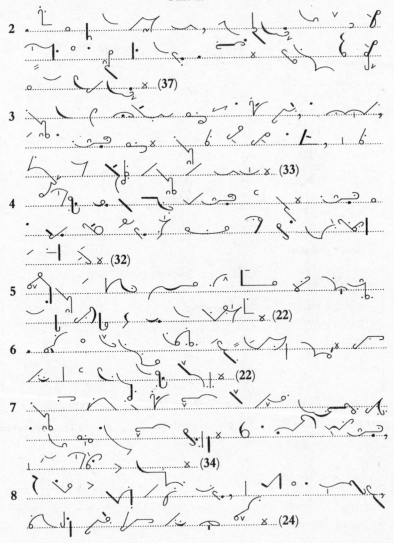

2 .... (37)

3 .... (33)

4 .... (32)

5 .... (22)

6 .... (22)

7 .... (34)

8 .... (24)

As strokes of unequal length must not be joined unless there is an angle at the point of junction, strokes are sometimes disjoined for the sake of legibility:

| attitude | irritated | substituted | institute | promptness | outfit |

Read the outlines and copy them several times. Then read the following sentences and write them several times from dictation.

Exercise 93

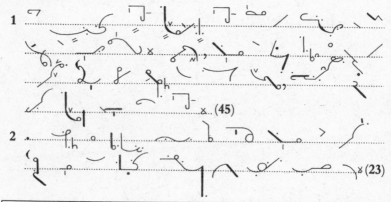

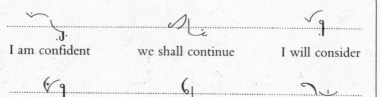

Short Forms

nevertheless	notwithstanding

Phrases

I am confident	we shall continue	I will consider
they will consider	this committee	very common

Read and write the above short forms and phrases several times before you read Exercise 94 and then write it from dictation.

Exercise 94

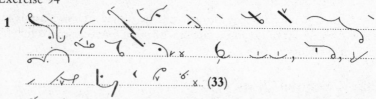

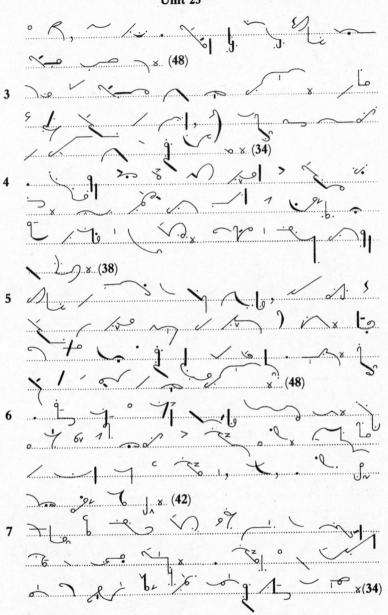

Short Form and Phrase Drill

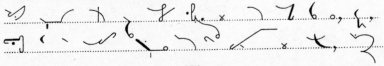

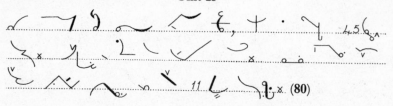

Exercise 95

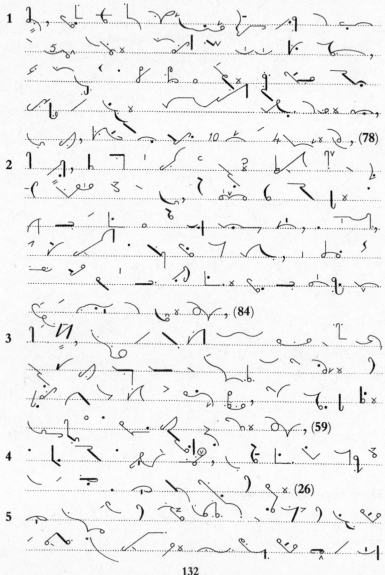

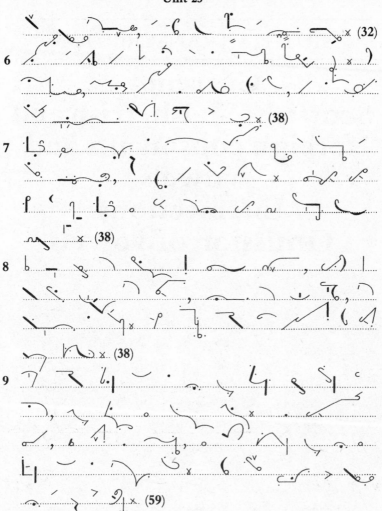

6

7

8

9

Currency
Scottish, Welsh, Irish and foreign consonants and vowels
Intersections
Omission of vowels

Currency may be expressed in the following ways:

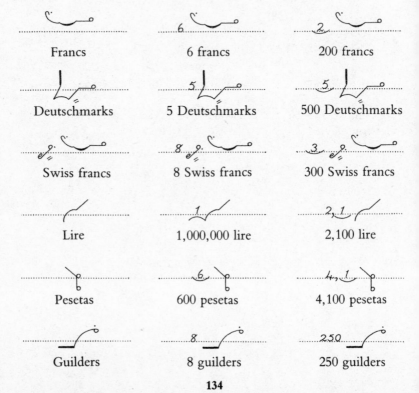

Francs	6 francs	200 francs
Deutschmarks	5 Deutschmarks	500 Deutschmarks
Swiss francs	8 Swiss francs	300 Swiss francs
Lire	1,000,000 lire	2,100 lire
Pesetas	600 pesetas	4,100 pesetas
Guilders	8 guilders	250 guilders

Scottish, Welsh and Irish consonants and vowels

The Scottish guttural *ch*, and the Irish *gh* are written:

ch ...., as in

loch   Lochaber

The Welsh *ll* by ...., as in:

Llan   Landaff   Llanelly

Foreign consonants and vowels

The German guttural *ch* is written .... as in:

ich   Dach

The French nasal *n* is written ...., as in:

soupcon   restaurant   entourage

Two similar French and German vowels are represented in the following way:

jeune   Goethe

Intersections

When a word to be indicated by an intersection is to be read first, the stroke representing the intersection is written first, and the outline for the following word is written through the stroke:

business world   company's profits   arranging parties

135

form enclosed　　　required charge　　　business associates

company regulations　　　corporation tax

When it is not possible to write an intersection through another stroke, proximity may be used:

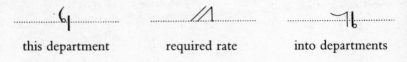

this department　　　required rate　　　into departments

Omission of Vowels

In Unit 21 reference is made to the omission of vowels and the insertion of essential vowels. The following are a few guide lines regarding the insertion of essential vowels.

Generally speaking, vowels should be inserted where words of the same part of speech have similar outlines and the same position for the outline; where a word is unfamiliar, or unfamiliar in the special sense in which it is used; where an outline has been written incorrectly, badly, or in the wrong position, in which case the insertion of a vowel is the quickest way of making the outline legible.

It is advisable to vocalize as fully as possible when the subject-matter is unknown.

The following lists contain some of the more common words in which the vowels indicated by italic type should be inserted in order to aid transcription:

Insertion of an initial vowel

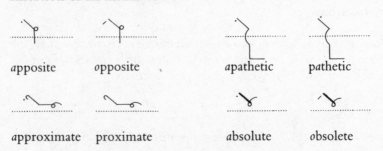

*a*pposite　　　*o*pposite　　　*a*pathetic　　　p*a*thetic

*a*pproximate　　proximate　　　*a*bsolute　　　*o*bsolete

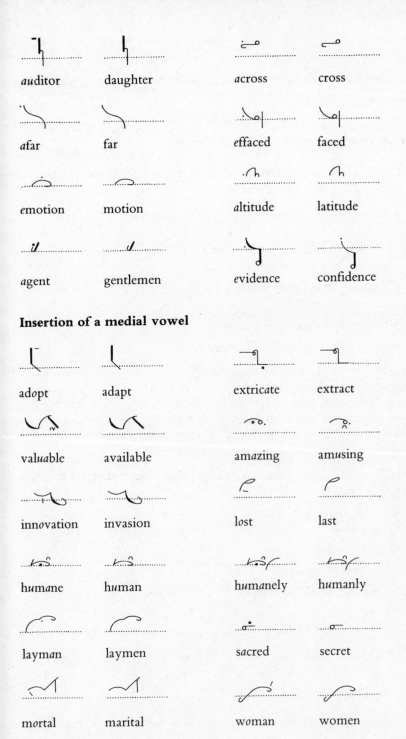

auditor

daughter

across

cross

afar

far

effaced

faced

emotion

motion

altitude

latitude

agent

gentlemen

evidence

confidence

Insertion of a medial vowel

adopt

adapt

extricate

extract

valuable

available

amazing

amusing

innovation

invasion

lost

last

humane

human

humanely

humanly

layman

laymen

sacred

secret

mortal

marital

woman

women

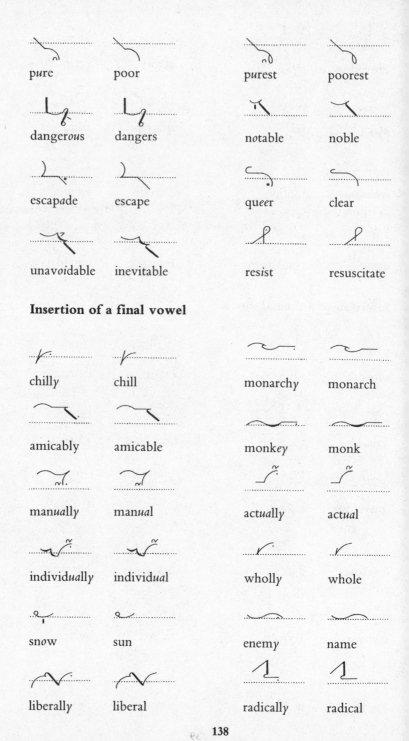

| pure | poor | purest | poorest |

| dangerous | dangers | notable | noble |

| escapade | escape | queer | clear |

| unavoidable | inevitable | resist | resuscitate |

Insertion of a final vowel

| chilly | chill | monarchy | monarch |

| amicably | amicable | monkey | monk |

| manually | manual | actually | actual |

| individually | individual | wholly | whole |

| snow | sun | enemy | name |

| liberally | liberal | radically | radical |

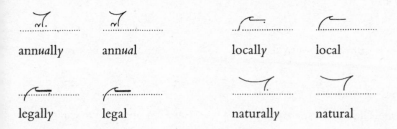

| annually | annual | locally | local |

| legally | legal | naturally | natural |

Transcription aids

In order to produce an exact transcription from shorthand notes, it is necessary to insert a vowel in some phrases or to write an outline in full in order to distinguish the formal from the colloquial:

| I am | I'm | you are | you're |

| we are | we're | he is | he's |

| she is | she's | that is | that's |

| I will | I'll | you will | you'll |

| he will | he'll | she will | she'll |

| they will | they'll | it will | it'll |

| I have | I've | you have | you've |

| they have | they've | I cannot | I can't |

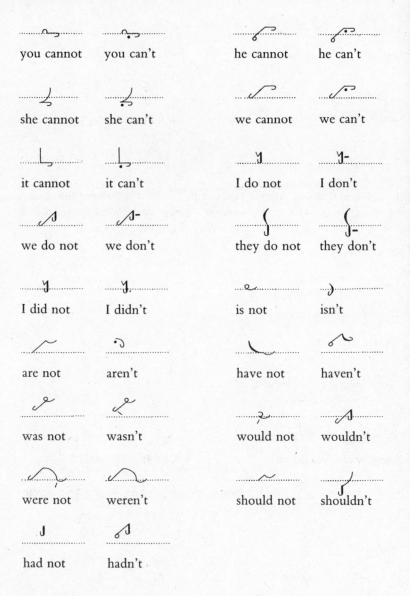

you cannot	you can't	he cannot	he can't
she cannot	she can't	we cannot	we can't
it cannot	it can't	I do not	I don't
we do not	we don't	they do not	they don't
I did not	I didn't	is not	isn't
are not	aren't	have not	haven't
was not	wasn't	would not	wouldn't
were not	weren't	should not	shouldn't
had not	hadn't		

In phrases, when the structure of two outlines is identical except for the vowels, distinction is obtained by inserting a vowel in one and omitting the vowel in the other:

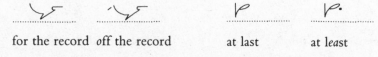

for the record	off the record	at last	at least

we say	we *see*	you can say	you can *see*
he can say	he can *see*	we can say	we can *see*
let us say	let us *see*	you will say	you will *see*
by any means	by *no* means	I give	I g*a*ve
we give	we g*a*ve	young man	young m*e*n
in another case	in n*ei*ther case	in any case	in *no* case
in any way	in *no* way	businessman	businessm*e*n

In order to avoid mistranscription, it is advisable not to join some outlines but to join others:

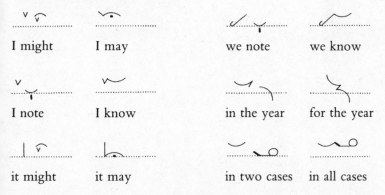

I might	I may	we note	we know
I note	I know	in the year	for the year
it might	it may	in two cases	in all cases

| it is not necessary | it is unnecessary | it is not natural | it is unnatural |

| it is not known | it is unknown | we are not able to | we are unable to |

Acronyms

When taking dictation it is important to record exactly what has been spoken. Occasionally, it may be necessary to write abbreviations and, generally, it is much easier to write these in lower case letters:

USA would be written ..... *usa* ..... UK would be written ..... *uk* .....

When the letters form acronyms, that is when they are pronounceable as words, it is better to write the sounds as they are spoken:

UNICEF NASA UNESCO

SHORT FORMS

Examples of **some** common derivatives are shown indented. Unit numbers indicated throughout.

a/an (**3**)		being (**3**)	
able to (**9**)		before (**20**)	
accord/according/ (**12**)		but (**4**)	
according to (**12**)			
accordingly (**18**)		cannot (**17**)	
all (**3**)		commercial/	
almost (**11**)		commercially (**20**)	
although (**8**)		could (**6**)	
always (**8**)		dear (**12**)	
also (**8**)		difficult (**22**)	
altogether (**20**)		difficulty (**22**)	
an/a (**3**)		do (**2**)	
and (**1**)		doing (**2**)	
any/in (**2**)		dollar/had (**7**)	
anybody (**13**)		enlarge (**21**)	
anyhow (**15**)		enlarged (**21**)	
anyone (**17**)		enlargement (**21**)	
anything (**2**)		enlarger (**21**)	
are (**5**)		enlarges (**21**)	
as/has (**4**)		enlarging (**21**)	
be (**3**)		eye/I (**2**)	
		first (**11**)	

for (3)

from (20)

gentleman (17)

gentlemen (17)

had/dollar (7)

has/as (4)

have (3)

having (3)

he (phrasing only) (15)

his/is (1)

hour/our (5)

hours/ours (5)

how (14)

I/eye (2)

immediate (11)

immediately (11)

in/any (2)

influence (10)

influenced (10)

influencing (10)

influential (21)

information (24)

is/his (1)

it (1)

its (2)

January (23)

knowledge (19)

acknowledge (19)

acknowledgement (19)

acknowledging (19)

large (7)

largely (9)

larger (12)

largest (11)

manufacture (5)

manufactured (5)

manufacturer (5)

manufactures (5)

manufacturing (5)

more (20)

Mrs (13)

nevertheless (25)

nothing (2)

notwithstanding (25)

of (1)

on (7)

ought (8)

our/hour (5)

ours/hours (5)

ourselves (5)

owe/oh (8)

owed (8)

Word		Word	
owes (8)		the (tick used in phrasing) (1)	
owing (8)		there/their (20)	
particular (12)		therefore (23)	
particularly (18)		thing (2)	
particulars (12)		anything (2)	
put (13)		nothing (2)	
puts (13)		something (2)	
putting (13)		think (6)	
responsible/ responsibility (17)		thinking (6)	
satisfaction (24)		thinks (6)	
satisfactory (20)		this (3)	
unsatisfactory (24)		to (1)	
several (10)		today (1)	
shall (7)		tomorrow (8)	
should (10)		to be (13)	
something (2)		together (20)	
subject (14)		too/two (2)	
subjected (14)		trade/toward (12)	
subjecting (14)		trades/towards (12)	
subjects (14)		trader (12)	
thank (3)		trading (12)	
thanked (4)		two, too (2)	
thankful (21)		unsatisfactory (24)	
thanking (3)		very (20)	
thanks (3)		we (4)	
that (6)		which (7)	

who (9)	......✓......	year (13)	......⌐......
will (4)	......⌐......	yesterday (4)	......⤸......
willing (4)	......⌐·......	you (2)	......o......
with (3)	c	your (5)	......⌐......
without (10)	......ᐸ......	yours (5)	......⌐......
wonderful/ wonderfully (23)	......⟋......	yourself (5)	......ᐱ......
would (6)	......ᴐ......		

INTERSECTIONS

arrange/arranged/
arrangement (**16**)
arranging (**16**)

attention (**24**)

business (**13**)

charge (**8**)

company (**12**)

company limited (**12**)

corporation (**24**)

department (**18**)

enquire/enquiry/
inquire/inquiry (**19**)

form (**8**)

month (**21**)

require/required/
requirement (**19**)

Circle S may be added to the intersections to indicate plurals or possessive case.

147

INDEX

Index